"Reading V. B. Price's latest colle... geode, revealing a dazzling array of poetic concerns. These poems contain fragments of experience, wisdom, and even conflict. Price's words are somehow both the hammer and the stone—and the heavy whack that splits the geode into radiant halves."

— **Amaris Feland Ketcham**, author of **Glitches in the FBI** and **A Poetic Inventory of the Sandia Mountains**

"This is a remarkable collection of poems capturing a dozen years where frailties and strengths are interwoven to create a rope from which hope and doubt hang together. *Así es la vida*, and Price's Selected Poems 2008–2020 reminds us that *even in the faintest ripple in the gravity of history we are, but we are not*. The collection's eloquence and articulation hum with the poetics of a life fully lived and do not look back in regret."

— **Levi Romero**, inaugural New Mexico Poet Laureate

"V. B. Price's poems remind us that beautiful construction is part of what makes reading poetry enjoyable. The craft of these poems, the sound, the syllable, the line, the shape and white space, create delight on every page while at the same time being transparent. We forget the technical and are lifted into a world where the mundane becomes magical and we are reminded to gasp and take in how lucky we are to be human and live in this world as we see it through his eyes."

— **Jonatha Kottler**, writer (The Guardian, Audible, Longreads) and teacher

"Humane, deep, joyful, feral, challenging, beautiful, and always always always welcome. V. B. Price is a better poet than we deserve."

— **Daniel Abraham**, co-author of the New York Times bestselling series **The Expanse**

Polishing the Mountain,
or
Catching Balance Just in Time

Other works by V. B. Price

Poetry
Innocence Regained: Christmas Poems
Memoirs of the World in Ten Fragments
Rome MMI
Broken and Reset: Selected Poems 1966 to 2006
Death Self (with Rini Price)
Mythwaking
Chaco Trilogy
The Seven Deadly Sins
Chaco Body
Documentaries
Semblances
The Cyclops' Garden

Nonfiction
The Orphaned Land
The University of New Mexico
Albuquerque: A City at the End of the World
Monsters (with Vincent Price)

Fiction
The Oddity

POLISHING THE MOUNTAIN

OR CATCHING BALANCE JUST IN TIME

SELECTED POEMS
2008-2020

V. B. PRICE

Casa Urraca Press
ABIQUIU

Cover painting, *Seven Trees*, by Rini Price.
Set in Century Schoolbook and Mostra Nuova.

24 23 22 21   1 2 3 4 5 6 7

First edition

Exclusive hardcover ISBN 978-1-956375-00-8
Paperback ISBN 978-1-7351516-8-7

CASA URRACA PRESS

an imprint of Casa Urraca, Ltd.
PO Box 1119
Abiquiu, New Mexico 87510
casaurracaltd.com

To Robin, Rini, Skip, Margaret, Barbara, Zach, Benito, and Mikki.

Contents

Introduction

It's been fifteen years since *Broken and Reset: Selected Poems 1966 to 2006* was published by the University of New Mexico Press. I was sixty-six years old and considered myself lucky to have lived so long. Now I am eighty-one and luckier than ever. I was surprised to find that in those intervening years I had composed seven new poem cycles, written thirteen Christmas poem suites, published a collection of some forty-three years of Christmas poems, and completed dozens of other poems. If I'm lucky enough to live a little longer, I could finish a long poem sequence that takes off from the Roman poet Lucretius' major work, *On the Nature of Things*, called The Logic of Venus. I also have hopes of completing a sequel to *Memoirs of the World* with the working title Planet Now.

The title of this book—*Polishing the Mountain*—comes from a prayer cycle I call Badger Ethics, a sequence of admonishments in answer to the plea "What do I do now?" that has evolved into a daily and calming meditative recitation. Trying to learn what to overlook, struggling to keep focused on what matters, catching myself when I fail to see purpose and order as the "refuge of now," and polishing away so I won't forget to "worry not," as the Badger admonished, has been for me like rubbing a smooth stone endlessly all over the surface of the Sandia Mountains with no expectation of results.

Catching Balance Just in Time refers to the precarious existence during the last decade or so that all of us have borne with climate change, political mayhem and madness which saw an actual insurrection and storming of the U.S. Capitol on January 6, 2020, and a global virus that kept us all in some form of quarantine for more than a year during the Covid pandemic. It was a precariousness that included the closing of the *Albuquerque Tribune* where I'd written for more than twenty years, and the ending of forty years of teaching seminars at UNM's Honors College and School of Architecture and Planning. It was a time that also saw the slow but inexorable dismantling through illness and death of my large extended family of friends, which culminated in my late wife, the artist Rini Price, being stricken with dementia, a worsening condition that continued over the last four and a half years of her life following the death of her sister. It was a time traversed by both of us on a saggy tightrope over a sulfurous gorge, catching balance over and over again, always just in time. Rini's gallantry, kindness, love, and gentle humor were the balancing pole that kept us from falling off.

When you struggle with the generous futility of polishing a mountain, you may find the beginnings of a shiny vein of good fortune. This happened to me in September 2020 when, with no warning obvious to me, my heart stopped beating—in my doctor's office. I was brought back to life, physically, by my doctor and his brilliant nurses, and, emotionally, by the grace of new love. I think now of what's ahead not as "gravy"—my whole life's been like that, mostly: delicious, rich, savory despite many blindsidings and my raft of failings—but as a field of exuberance and spontaneous, overwhelming gratitude that catches me by surprise with its beauty at every turn.

Polishing the Mountain,
or
Catching Balance Just in Time

For Mary and Kit on Their Wedding Day

To marry:
to constellate,
stars in a commons,
common gravities
free in space so true
no light rubs wrong
no other light.
So too this dance,
this grace, this perfect, fine
true freedom spun
and drawn so close.
The best is always
one and two
free and forever freer
in the holy dark,
aligned each upon all,
the trust of fun
never drained:
the vast mystery
of being happy
two and one on one.

(2008)

Steering with Your Knees

I.

Ambition all sopped up, fear moths
yawning in the closet far away,
old luck completed; you've raised yourself
to be who you are, now you want just a message
you can trust and quiet days
sleepy with being. Is this what's left
to someone who's kept alive by his wits,
and pitiless, flat trabajo, missing no luck
when it showed its head, like a worm in a fire storm?
The hand in the dark is cool with joy.
You have always been who you're meant to be.

II.

Sleep smudging through life,
how can it not be hard to wake up?
A day is a smear, the world itself
an eyelash in the eye, the brain field
parqueted with goatheads. Wake up.
Isn't consciousness holy thrift?
Joy slipping around the corner.
To hell with the demons.
Pour smiles on them and get out of the way.
You don't want to watch them melting.

III.

The Oracle spoke through the winds
and choppy shadows of the grievous woods.
You have no other duty.
Tell the story the other way.
You are a safe place to be.

IV.
Loyalty to old trowels, and hoes, and shovels—
you know their meaning, you have stemmed in them
the flow of departing and forgetting,
made them as real as you are
in the field of yourself, as much a part of you
as your good habits are.
Carry your file while you're weeding.
Everything needs its own kind of love.

V.
It all falls away
once the inner solipsist
frolics off down the beach
into the blackening deep
where friction mingles
with the lightning air;
and when you've let it
out the door and return
to your breakfast table
with its papers, books,
jars of pens, the day
of your life can continue
as if it were what it is
just a day to unfold and be
what it turns out to be.

VI.
When the brain's blackness
becomes a comfort and refuses to be
a freezing absence, and when shadows
become companions, and death is not
an emptiness stuffed with depression
and dying is just a long view to move into
making it our cherished passage
when love becomes gray haired
and gorgeous in its kindness,
then the cold enamel table
of dissection and the scalpels of the cynic
just slide off into the beautiful pond
lost without a splash.

VII.
Her ashes in the ground:
Strawberry Roan,
sunfishing, riderless, forever.
She's just one. So many
dead or going,
old mentors and gods;
hardly anyone left but us.
What are we losing?
Their generosity
is in us, their faith in us
is us. What are we losing?
Ourselves, eroding away
into a new geography without us.

VIII.
When you're content to be weathered
by your life, you become what you've been given
and the life you have chosen day after day.
You are what has happened, what you don't
understand as much as what you trust, your calm,
your life of agitation that propels you.
You are what has kept you alive and what will,
as clouds are always moving, always clouds,
and all their chances missed and to be.

IX.
You can tell when you've been seen
with total sight, everywhere mysteries opening,
no one left behind, life free as it is, no exceptions.
When you're seen like that, you can live your life
the way freedom has organized itself, let's say, in the body,
in historical time and place, in culture, but you can't
change the incline or wobble anywhere. You see them
coming and try, for as long as your body can,
to be agile enough to dance away
from the fissures and jumping boulders falling anywhere
all around you. And when you can't, you will be
as gracious, courtly, calm and thrilled
as you've been all through the light fantastic.

X.
Allowing,
you *are*
what's next,
free
as greeting
a welcoming,
beloved
full body.
This is so
with the universe
of fire and death and animals
with unique,
personal ways
shrieking in the jaws
of their fate.
Allowing is more
than accepting.
It's giving yourself
to your life, with no
taking back,
as it comes to you.
It's more than not
minding pain.
It's allowing,
which is
to chance
what attention is
to mind.

XI.
The luckless mob; stained and oily,
dust hair wadded, lint and pubic curl nasty,
urine-cake world you'd never lick up by choice,
this is what your heart must open to, open as it does
to roses, to dill forests with lolling cats
and sweet beer highs in the twilight with summer heat
lifting off, cooling in its parting the sweaty creases of your worry.

XII.
If you don't know where you come from
you will always be a child, Cicero says.
Baffled, without bearing, tossed
on the squall mind with its swamping dreads,
perfect storms of resentment, you will never see past
the playroom's foggy windows. If you do know, though,
if you've cleared the steam from a small edge of the pane,
just enough to see some rushing of the countryside
turning from one blur into another, you have come
to the point of seeing experience at least,
which is the first step into the fields of who you are,
now that you've left where you came from and are starting back.

XIII.
Remembering my own first time
knowing through my body,
with no text, no scripture, no teaching,
life's delight in itself in me,
the greater joy, with no
yes or no, just all trust that's free
as a bird is free to fly, a cat to lounge,
a lizard to rustle up its own game of tag.

XIV.
We have to believe in the gods we trust
in the same way we know the gnarl
of meteorite, the black seashell with its silver swirling tip,
the whale-gray stone with its red jasper ridge,
know the round sand planet sitting like Saturn
in a limestone circle. They are real,
and more than we can explain or describe,
even after spending years writing of the meteoritic glob
smoothed by friction, we create only a flaw-shadow,
a decoy of its truth, the same for explaining why
some gods are real and others are not,
even if all are true.

XV.
New Year: waking in the middle of the night,
snow sliding off the roof, ears pounding,
Saddam approaching the gallows,
"just giving up" to the noose.
The futility of wild supposes,
limbs falling, roofs caving like trapdoors
falling open to the endless sky.
Where am I? "You are what you do."
"You are what you think you are."
When you carry martinis on a silver tray,
it's best not to focus on the wavering gin.

XVI.
Brain footed in concrete,
ego wiggling nowhere,
he should have kept it moving,
let the roof drain, the blood pulse,
the money flow out so
it won't add up to the world's suffocation.
"Next time," he hissed, choking on diamonds.
He knew what's needed is never
too little, but better too much
than too fast, too big, too slow, too hobbled.
Just right is an all-time profession
and better than spending your life
trying not to tip over.

XVII.
Who you are forever
is in who you are right now,
not that forever is a given.
The test is how to put now
together with always,
this time with the endless once,
eachness with forever. When we learn
who we always are, resting there,
without waste or forgetting,
now and forever dissolve, the island
shudders and decides not to sink,
the preacher takes up canning and the cat
won't stop yapping about this and that.

XVIII.
The horrors that could befall us:
the prankster's bucket of cold piss
poised to spill from the top of the door
when we open it with unsuspecting habit.
They are all in there, like eyeballs and goiters
in the bouillabaisse—microbes, asteroids,
Hitler, stroke, the guilt of your life revealed,
guilt that is no more who you are
than the grapefruit-sized tumor
on top of your spine. All you can do
is check each door for a bucket,
and maybe wear a bucket on your head
and carry a plunger for a sword, in case
it's your mind that's the toilet.

XIX.
Sailing along making poems
on a conveyor-belt river
of slick ball bearings, oily rattles,
guns, old sofas, nano silver grease on socks,
almost tumbling, almost rolling, almost
the waiter slipping on an oyster
with a full tray of tall drinks
in Empire glasses bearing the great
seal of the Czar of All the Russias
and then some. Not so terrible as it seems
—erasers, smoother than glassy booze,
go all the way around the page
removing every tumble, like a supplicant
can never be refused if help is fated.
If not, there's always maybe yes, maybe no.

XX.
On Job's planet, the atmosphere
is in layers of euphoria, torment,
exquisite boredom—
the stratigraphy of paradox
builds like Babble to the sky.
Some live whole lives
in layers of homey dilapidation,
some in layers of domestic acid. Some
are satisfied with a good cup of coffee,
others can't wait to die.
Is there any common fate
where comradery rests?
Life, not its scathing,
is the common ground, isn't it?
And thanks-never-ending the only rescue.

(2008)

Bolt Upright

I.
Ruinations
of talent, indecision
feeding
sloth, sloth
soothing doubt, doubt
fidgeting skill, skill
breaking apart, a comet
hitting depression.
Ruinations
of chance, lost
pains
unconverted,
blessings trapped
with smears in drains,
genius careening
into self-loathing, ricocheting
off hoops papered over
with three a.m. jottings.
The luckily endowed
petered out
in habits beyond regretting,
Edens
compromised, embodied
as ivy vines
tripping up
an old man with a basket of laundry
who breaks his crown
on a pointed stone
in a graveyard for cats
who never looked out
for his interests.

II.
It is unavoidable.
Little mattered but her anymore, her
and their mythological life.
They were movie house cutouts
to most everyone else, even the best.
Dwelling on his mother's
tragedy over lunch
would be to most
like spending weeks exhuming
shoelaces, mass graves of frogs, or gluing
a brittle rubber band
into a condom.

The mythic world of firsts,
first smell of pines,
first love of skin, first betrayal,
the poems of our rapture,
these are all behind them, as theirs were
beyond him but not
quite... at least he looked
at the shadows
in their caves, he listened
out of courtesy
and some curiosity,
and a spare few of them
listened, too, now and then,
when he'd sensed
through the Labyrinth
they might be,
and stepped out to say
something true
in front
of the curtain of Oz.
He refused
to beg for attention.

III.
He trips on a step.
She spills the tea.
The cat's unnerved,
the tomatoes are quite
unconcerned
by the color red.
He's tired when he gets up in the morning.
His shoes filled with silt
and nothing is less
than it seems.
So he removes
the top portion
of a cornice and finds
a key that opens a door
in the next village
in a house that was
destroyed by a flood
and everything that used to make sense
still does. But now
it's not enough.

IV.
Sometimes nothing happens
when it should. Leaves don't fall.
Cranes are late. The cat chases
the wily bird up a tree
and tries to fly after it.
Snow comes down as gruel.
Sometimes it's all spot on.
The truck plows into the car;
the bird drops its load with an apple seed
in the back corner of your garden;
the wiser one in your life
hears you wrong and thinks
you've caught on at last.
Timing is everything, we're told,
usually by someone who's
beaten us to the punch.

V.
What a bore. The world is
as it is:
famine, murder,
peaceful nights,
torture, plague,
exquisite love;
and we
are as we are,
burning ants,
whole landscapes,
whole generations
if we could,
with the magnifying glass
of sentience, caught not
in demon glee,
but in how
we are made,
consciousness always
conscious
of something, which is
always us.
We can do little about
the roiling of joy with catastrophe,
as helpless in the world of tsunamis
and normal horrors
as we are in the world
of our bodies, except
we can heal *them*
by a simple change
of the lens
of belief.

We are always free to practice
the states we believe to be good,
that is
as we are,
free to aspire, not minding,
maybe yes, maybe no,
but the yes—that's worth
all the difference.

VI.
Even falling
out of grace
falls within
the field of grace,
all embraced.
Even the staining
of peace is cleaned
when time, full
of its debris,
softens minds, so all
is forgotten
and forgiveness stays
unneeded.
The purity of *is*
is the rock,
a grace
even fate
cannot erase. *Is,*
whole and all, *is*
is the calm, sane
without exception,
pause or flaw,
the nothing
that is all,
all ways, always,
all before it's here,
all before it's gone.

VII.
The brilliant nibbling
of piranha-like minds
doing what they think,
just skimming,
taking the sole morsel
from the starving girl's plate
and nodding kindly that yes
her hunger is what she gets.
There they go,
the pious takers,
rough-riding
through the eyes
of needles
on camels greased
with porno
compassion,
swarming on
heaven, their jaws
nipping while paws
of the cosmos
morally squash
their insatiable self-
righteous choice
of themselves,
relentlessly made
inconsequential
in the end.

VIII.
Glued by gravity
gone feral and obese,
smashed flat by shock
on the yellow and pink
linoleum floor, face down
before the toilet,
the death wish
heaving with a thrill,
he felt the first
freezing of hope
and groaned to lift
one finger
then another, each one
a hundred pounds, but he
pried himself up
with the leverage
of his will,
the audacity
not to mind,
and finally moved
to finish his life,
the book, the dreams,
the pleasures that make
gravity a caress;
it was all, as they say,
in his mind. What
did it matter now
that the sickle
was toppling them all
at the ankles?

IX.
We don't know.
But we're steering.
Will the inner
douser take us on
both forks of the tongue?
It doesn't matter;
meaning's destination
is the same
in name only.
Our most
permanent contribution,
poorly recorded
with many missed words
in the failing minds
of those regarded
as experts
on texts they've warped
to remember as their own—
is this our
posthumous existence?

X.
He devoted himself
to his interests,
refusing to surface beyond
the field of his fine curiosity.
Why shouldn't he?
Don't others have
such terrors, was he
the only one afraid
of tipping over
and falling off,
wasn't everyone just
a misstep away,
disease and oppression
loose rugs on the long
slick hall of mirrors?
The misstep didn't
even have to be his.
Was he the only one
burying his heart
in his puzzles, toy soldiers,
collections of dwarf
Persian rugs?
Was he the only one
who couldn't survive
without his distractions?
If he was a coward
in a room full of cowards
did that really matter to him?
Oh no. It did.

XI.
He understood
practice works,
that years of trying
lead to something,
that the brain
changes, that bad habits
can be replaced,
that you can
learn to say
the alphabet backwards,
can recall the word
for bacon in Spanish, can
keep growing, can
keep getting saner, more
proficient, happier even.
But what
gives you the will
to want to?
Even the outhouse man,
untouchable,
at the end of the line,
with no hope at all,
bows to that.

XII.
Nightmare tossing,
face down in a pond,
unable to surface,
knowing the next
breath he takes
will drown him,
and he breathes
and awakes
to asteroids gouging out Kansas,
tortures leaving her strung up,
rotator cuffs screaming, while they
stroll off to lunch and a good conversation;
a dirty bomb smeared over Manhattan; goose-stepping
agents in his living room at three a.m.
marching all over his naked toes.
They are
all as they are,
of course, but they are
nothing except
what he makes of them;
they are not, in fact,
and his response to nothing
is still his.
He is
the dungeon
under the rug.

If it is mine, he thought,
why not replace it
with what I want?
Why not?
Inside he felt
desires are
openings, dreads
rusted closings.
If neither
are real, his last
chance is
don't go there,
go somewhere else,
look the other way,
overlook, turn
to morning land,
the breakfast nook,
hot toast, jam,
the screen door
slamming open,
slapping shut
far behind you.

(2009)

Chaco Nights

The stars were his;
he'd breathed them in.

The Milky Way inside
was all around him,

a respiration of the night.
He had seen the Otherside

without idea, more beautiful
behind its veils of meaning,

invisibly far but known
like the stone in his pocket.

Who had let him in?
Why now at the stub of his life?

He'd been shown
how to climb the crevasse

to the top
where nothing

is what it is
because the *is*

is infinite. Yes,
he had felt

the great door opening,
night pouring into his lungs,

star streams in the dark
through the bay of his mind,

the night river full
of every sun

of every dawn rise
in the universe.

He knew he wasn't
dying yet.

Many friends were gone,
many wiping their shoes

on the welcome mat of the end.
His turn would come around.

Cancer? Heart attack? Who knows?
Latvians, in a little town

on the border, hanged their Cleansed
from lamp posts, twenty of them

(it was a small town),
before the Nazis invaded

and stole all their stuff.
Cancer, who knows?

Auto wreck, some terrible
slippage?

Who can second-guess
the last of the strange

revelations?
Of course,

Pain and Fear are tricksters.
They guide us to desert them;

hang onto their tails for the ride,
but don't crawl

into their skins.
They're already in them.

They *will*
serenely deign to destroy you.

Something else must come to us
from the night,

from the quaking,
the dread supposings.

Something else
must open us wide,

roll us out
onto the cold, far road

to the Otherside, straight
as a thought can make it,

from nowhere to nowhere,
from lives of cowering

in desire, cowering
in the norm, praying it won't

fall away and leave us
falling through the spaces.

Something else must open us wide
to climb from cowering in caution, up

the spine of the mind
into the night and its skeleton of stars,

climbing up into the currents
of the fecund nothing

forever ending, never over,
the space among the fires,

dark as the far end of it all,
with yes

everywhere we look,
bright as the fog of stars

exhaled into the night
and breathed back in

to the wholly ambiguous peace
in the deepest trust of our bodies.

(2010)

Memento Mori

It is so old
it's witnessed dust
begetting dust:
that shrine of codes

where, unerased,
demand still reads:
Know Thyself
if you dare;

if you don't,
don't expect to know
what you know.
Self mirrors all

it sees: sea foam
rushing, refreshing corpses
on Omaha Beach,
dogs racing

surf, babies
giggling at Poseidon,
amniotic
paradise, a killing

pool almost:
placenta starved,
half dead, born
a refugee so small

I'm swaddled tight,
a prisoner of my saviors,
brain big by the grace
of oxygen, undeflated,

devils twisting neurons
garroting someone else.
Born empty, no
gyroscope, no

guiding stars,
no scent of future
consequence,
we wake up one day

stunned at the danger
of being loved.
In the mulch of grief
his fame

a cold deep shadow
stunting growth,
his perfection
an explosion

of standards
imposed but set
only for him to meet.
Why should it surprise us

to learn we are unique
and common,
irreplaceable
and expendable,

pleasure lusting
in minds of pain,
tickled by
the teasing love

of magic beauty
until we puke—Dead
Horse Point
standing for the edge

of trust as we know it.
It's such a shock to us to be
so unimportant
in our momentousness:

rejections on
industrial scales—
best jokes, books,
drawings, compost

for allies and even mentors.
It's such a shock
that the world
would rather we not

clog the drain
with our meaning and our
fastidious
tenaciousness:

Mexico City students
slipping and smeared
in the blood that was once
in the bodies of their friends,

candy skulls and Castro,
a wedding of superstitious
politics, mustard seeds and
cynics' digs at truth:

the strange one, son,
denied intelligence
and forbidden to be
useful more than freakish.

It's not our fault
we were born
rich or poor, prone
to neurosis,

angst, crippled
by genius or privilege
or malnutrition, forced
to overcome our talents

and our flaws.
It's not our fault that we die
choked up with crud or eaten
to death by our cannibal cells.

We are the managers
of our firefly lives,
we tend our destinies,
our infinitesimal

flashes
in the pan,
with only hope for the best
as a guide

with no experience. It's
those unwelcome prophet
dreams, as much
as chance,

that make us who we are:
Awakening
from a horrormare
of sloth, I'd seen

the end days of my life
and felt I had
wasted it all
by not

working and working
hard enough. Now my life
is so callused I can't
keep anything on me

clean enough to be seen.
And only now, so late,
when we see our memory
beautiful and false,

and our opinions
about ourselves just
wildcard guesses,
only now

when we see
we are one
of an infinity
of perishable

absolutes, like mother was:
a Belsen stick corpse
in a Bambi world,
pure genius of course,

without effect, always
trying, ever ending up
caught in a tragic
kink in the flow,

her sibylline friend
mute in the noose
of her terrible
abject no;

only now
do we understand
that knowing ourselves is
an antiquarian pursuit,

looking for the provenance
of why,
learning all there is to know
about Gaul

except where it is, or everything
about a pit house in the desert
except who built it, every detail
about that calyx

with the magnificent
indecipherable god.
It's beyond us that the world
is as it is,

that people would push
other people naked
from airplanes
in the frozen night

into the tar-black sea, that Lorca
would be hauled to a gully
and shot low down dead,
that he would have had

Santa Euelia's
"smoking breasts"
to write about—
so shockingly

beyond us,
so horrible
our beloved world—
we would die for it

as it's killing us.
This commonness! Even so,
our gnat lives don't
make us buzzing rubbish.

The mysterious
is in us. We ask for help
and are obliged with answers
that never go away.

We cannot
take ourselves apart
and put ourselves
back together alive.

Nanking, Sand Creek,
Babi Yar, puppet corpses,
strings tying up
bricks of cash. We are

insurmountably
dense. Like geographies
move without motion—
roiling, swelling, uplifting,

exploding, buckling, cascading
in their verity—their immeasurable
inconsistency rolling
out of the logic

of cause and effect,
it is fathomless to us, just as it's
not possible for us to see
the gates of yes and no

whirring in the inner
confines of our times.
So it is when we first
comprehend we are not

the same,
and connive to hide
the difference
replacing bbbbbbs

and pppppps
with mmmmmmmmmms
and lllllllls
only to find they stick

to the palate
like peanut butter glue
too. And so we see
that who we are

and who we appear to be
are not the same;
our appearance
is not our substance,

and we then
begin to live
free of the foul
trickiness in the faux

sanity of society, explorers
with healthy personas
who disguise themselves
as who they really are.

We learn to stick to what we know,
the indelible,
that we were loved
poorly, profoundly

wrong,
perfectly
pure, as if
we were someone else;

it doesn't matter.
It is
what the Holy
Is did.

Mother's nightmare spiral
gave us who we are
in the fortitude
we deny we have.

For some it's clear:
two tasks: mastering how
to ride out fear, not tame it,
not break it, but not

bucked off it,
riding it:
an unbearable risk
that must be taken

or we die like cities
going blank.
And the other,
demanded

by the smothering
dream of sloth,
to never stop
inventing, never

turn our backs
on what's inside
ready to come out
on the page, like a saved

exhalation, at home
with skulls and stones,
low yellow light,
books and pens,

keeping the oasis
pure, where *cannot*
never interferes.
Those two, so delicately

almost impossible,
they are the Pegasus and Sleipnir,
they are the horses of the plains.
Some delusions

are indispensable.
We never doubt
the vault will open,
we just don't have an invitation

to the streaming of the muses.
When we discover our hidden life
is inescapable,
as much who we are

as who we want to be,
we are unlocked, not
transformed into miracles
of fulfillment,

but the big door comes ajar,
we read our own works
in the craw of the night
and cry seeing evidence

of interventions
not our own,
but of us, even if
with the rarest of the rare

of our true companions
we can only
stroll along with them inside
the hidden life, pointing out

that monument and this dark strata,
this pile of notes, this lost delight.
And even we, sometimes,
in our inner world

are Alices shrinking and towering
unable to be
of it and fully there
where homesickness never

finds its way home
and the anvil
of our moral struggles
rings out beneath the groans

of public right and wrong.
It is there we must risk
what actually
appeals to us,

stones ringed with meaning,
interstellar rivers,
the lives of poets on the lam,
what makes sense to us,

kindness, kindness,
kindness, not
the dicing
revelations of others,

but the mystery
we know without concept
that made, by rote,
our chances

one of a kind,
and us unique
as the vessels
of our chances,

instruments
designed to play
in the orchestra of minds:
and mine

so like father's,
curiosity
the fun of our lives,
profusions of orchids,

of masks and color fields,
liking what we know,
skulls of pumas,
badgers with prophetic gaits,

shells with their vaginal pinks,
us eager for a lunch at Giverny
in the daisy-yellow dining room, even while
he curses himself

for fumbling
his wonderful life,
his mind most happy,
sore, self-digesting

and unfulfilled, the model
of who I did
not want to be,
my hero without

knowing it, my in-
frequent guide, my
honored pal, not
my benchmark.

"Fortune's child," he called me.
She said to me, sober
from gin's concerned relief,
"Get out of your way,

get out of your shadow."
Shadowless on my back porch
I have my beer and talk
the universe with the pure

blooded love of my life,
still stunned that someone
dark and forbidden
as I am should have it all

from the Venus of everything,
whose shadow stunts
and overawes all horrors.
Know thyself, she demands,

even if you can't
remember how you die,
just your shadowing terrors
of dying's knock

on the door while you're
dead asleep. And if the gods come clean,
knowing thyself, they agree,
is a mirage

hiding the end,
like a thin
paper wall
hides lovers

from the street,
or pure white lies
hide whatever is
too actual to know.

(2010)

from

Homeric America

(2011–2018)

NOTE: These poems are evocations of forty-eight Americans, twenty-four warriors and twenty-four wanderers who have a Homeric quality to their lives—forceful, adventurous, ill-fated, but fulfilled and heroic in their ways both Illiadic and Odyssean. I have chosen to write about formative people not as objects of biography or exposition, but as human fields of life, close to myths, which are themselves similar in experience to places and landscapes, describable in only the broadest terms, but available to anyone's firsthand inspection. William James's view of philosophy is much the same as our view of the memories we have of the people who have formed us, in person or through words: "No philosophy can ever be anything but a summary sketch, a picture of the world in abridgement, a foreshortened bird's-eye view of the perspective of events." We experience others largely by the effect they have on us as evolving personalities.

The Warriors: Robinson Jeffers (1887–1962)

Rapture and rage, dear Muses, help me sing
of this stone lover, this American hawk, alone and adored
in his tower, cursing and blessing, despised and loathing,
warring and never backing down.

Outside the outside, outcropped on the edge
of herd mind on the move, still as a boulder before it falls,
his loyalty feral to the bone, Jeffers withdrew
to "the trans-human magnificence" at continent's end,

a dog soldier tied to his pen, as America settled
into the "mold of its vulgarity"
and came to refuse him as he refused to thicken
into a lackey citizen of the sentimental mob.

He thought we are flawed, one of God's mistakes,
an omnivore cannibal self-devouring.
But what about him?
The flawed condemning the flawed.

He got the big picture as it is,
the stars don't care, and we're just
drops of gore in the cosmos. But he missed
the little picture, a Samson char-eyed to compassion.

It is single lives that matter, ennoble, transcend,
not species. Only squint thinkers judge
each of us by their opinion of all of us.
All of us are always at the edge,

history balanced so finely
if anything changes, the whole palace
of changeless progress falls
into chaos and social crime, elites

and their dull money skinning
the poor for their pelts, Arête gone punk
as he and Cassandra knew, civilization
crumbling on its rubbish and broken backs,

on excellence too frail to carry its own baggage.
He had no need to be liked, none for agreement. He knew
what he thought exactly. "Stark violence is still
the sire of all the world's values."

He knew his logic, his disgust, justified
his way of life: a Greek mind in an American time
of assembly-line gossip, paint-by-numbers moral wars
that bored even their victims, a mind that saw

everything turn on itself, all goodness marred,
as if Narcissus poisoned the well all the way
to the roots of each of us, his diagnosis
like the sick eco-joke unspoken in complaints

of overpopulation. That's the problem alright,
but a wrong that can't be fixed without
the ruination of billions of souls
isn't worth the mention.

In him we see man's insignificance to man.
"Not man apart." He was right.
Divorced from nature we are
a monstrosity, like him divorced

from a common bond. It did him in.
He didn't mind. One day he was
a *Time* magazine poet hero, a gaunt ideal,
the next compared to Tokyo Rose

or Ezra Pound in perfidy,
all for condemning a war
we won. But "Personal greatness
was never more than... a halo of illusion."

The Double Axe did it... "bloody slime,
all the dogs in the kennel   ।
killing one dog," the patriots howling,
censoring his howling, the Perishing

Republic's honored bums rush, shoving him
from the marketplace of acceptable folly.
"The strong struggle for power, and the weak
warm their poor hearts with hate."

But "Nothing is not alive.... The Hills dissolve... the stars
shine themselves dark." The "inhumanist" is not
a sadist. He's not a species narcissist. Nothing special.
He wanted us in our place,

along with the foxes, slime molds,
the adders, and the apes. In that he was
a minimalist, minimizing us.
He had trouble with the species,

the past piling up behind him, dead ideas
like hair that won't stop growing, until he turned
and blew away all pomp and conquest.
There was nothing of the salesman in him.

Of course he was marginal
by choice, an excluder, excluding everyone,
wanting everyone to exclude him. "Finally,
in white innocence the fighter planes like swallows dance..."

and the darkness before the last straw came.
He could hear the screams in the cockpits.
The wild swan wouldn't take him on its back.
He didn't expand like an Alice Joan d'Arc

and poke the tyrant's buttock with a number two pencil.
The tragic sense of life was not for him.
Only perfection has a tragic flaw,
the flawed are merely flawed, and therein is

redemption; but he missed it.
No theology covered his back.
Life devours; death devours.
All is hungry, time-famished,

flesh must be fed. No tragedy in fire,
no flaw in feeding and mistaking,
in hawks yanking feathers, a dove's
head eaten alive through the eyes.

Only the Ego thinks it deserves
what the Wild God of the World
withholds from the arrogant every time.
Grim follies can't be escaped by the proud.

The "rejection of human solipsism,"
the race becoming an adult rather than an
"egocentric baby or insane person"—that
goal was the only way for him to maintain

"sanity in slippery times," living his wits
that told him a "reasonable detachment"
was the best "rule of conduct, instead of love
hate or envy," all to neutralize

"fanaticism and wild hopes."
Not that the "magnificence"
is not to be adored. It is.
But he was a monist, an Either/Or

gnawer, with no place for And,
with no scent for the other side.
James wouldn't have stood for it.
But he would have stood with him

when it came to war feeding nothing,
from which nothing grows, no Eros
seeding the future, only Thanatos
digesting all roots.

Who can honestly say
he was completely wrong about us?
Big things like species are easy to track
—genocide, MAD, tactical famine, the Stasi,

COINTELPRO, Jim Crow, the tapeworm
of hate woven through the vestments of religion.
It's the details, like us, like minds and inner selves
that defy despair, that help us to see, as he saw,

"the excesses of God," who "flings
rainbows over the rain," and makes
"the necessary embrace of breeding,
beautiful also as fire," who sees

the "great humaneness at the heart of things,
the extravagant kindness" in guileless beauty,
but who knows "justice and mercy
are human dreams," belonging not

to the "birds nor the fish nor eternal God."
Is everything in the cosmos natural
but us? Are human dreams detached,
not as matter-of-fact as feathers

and scales, and pestering thoughts
of eternal love that scathes and maims as it licks and purrs?
How can anything be less existent
than everything else? Even an ashen cynic in denial

is as real as leaves and dust.
A return to life is the only answer,
to put our arms up to the elbows in cold, clear water,
no longer "a little too abstract, a little too wise,"

our campfires full of stories of joy, or the torturer's
red-hot iron. The ayes have it or they don't,
the swallows burn to the ground or dart off,
the hawks die too slowly or lift to the clouds,

the mountains crash like waves or soar
with the love of the gods. It is not
completely up to us, but to what else
but our thoughts can we appeal?

NOTE: Robinson Jeffers died at the age of seventy-five in 1962 at Tor House, twelve years after the death of his wife, Una. Tor House was built by him of beach stones and boulders near Carmel, California, overlooking the Pacific. He witnessed the Korean War during his early years of grief but missed the insertion of American combat troops into Vietnam in 1965. His great fame as a writer of American epic poems, as an "environmental icon," and as the translator of Euripides' *Medea* was virtually covered over by the fallout from his 1948 book *The Double Axe and Other Poems*, which was strongly anti-war and took a profoundly critical view of American intervention in World War II. Jeffers was portrayed as a dangerous crank, too radically detached from the mainstream of a victorious country to be considered anymore as one of its great poetic voices. Jeffers spoke truth to power, and power turned off his microphone.

The Wanderers: William James (1842–1910)

Flow through me, dear Muses, with ideas of this man
of the many and the pointed few, this voyager
through the mind-soul's twistings and turnings, always
simultaneous, true and free, and far, far seeing.

"The nobler thing tastes better, that's all we can say."
What else do we need to know?
                                        We wear down.
                                        The cosmos does that.
Our duty
            is to build up
            as we wear away.

Nothing doesn't matter. Each
is secured
            by each and all. Inclusion
stretches toward
the true,
exclusion shrinks
back,
            goes dark, falls morbid.
                                        "The whole
                                        preferred," James vowed. All of it,
the stagnant, strange,
the joyous and the rude,
what we understand
and what we never will.
                        All our troubles, pains,
uncertainties,
soften us up
                for freedom
                from one way thinking, the slamming door
of political illness.

At home with happiness. That
                              is magnet law. It attracts us.
                              Pleasure works. Yes is
                              stronger than no.
We "live on chance." There are
"real losses
            and real
            losers." But what's
                              "poured off the dregs
is sweet enough to accept."
                              Is there any doubt
the cosmos is pragmatic?
What doesn't work
isn't.
        It's just not.
                        Whatever works, it skirts
around dreamed-up truths
                              imposed like scripture,
                              graffiti script
marring the perfection
of what is always
                    pure experience before
                    the falling and the doubting.

The best philosophy
is the simplest. The one we trust
and understand the most is "our
                              more or less dumb sense
of what life honestly
and deeply means."
                    E pluribus unum: Philosophy
from the bottom up,

each of us learning
to be filled
and ripened by
                        our widest selves
in the "rich thicket of reality"—the spectrum
of the cosmos open to our brains
is well within the range of black to blank
and darker gray, indeed
                    like my cat's comprehension
                    of my library, books and maps,
                    or my comprehension
                    of his sleeping wiffles.

We don't need to know what we can't.
If thoughts make things
and feelings in the briar patch,
                        what's the use
                        of having a philosophy of life
                        that's not
"friendly and genial"
to the best variation of who we can be,
a philosophy
                intimate with possibility, vital
                with good chances
to help us sidestep the bull
of the "tremendous irrationalities" of the universe,
moving us toward the better and better
in the wise agility
                of a wider self
                that's ours
                and more?

What works
replaces what doesn't,
or gives it new life
                    as with the seeming
                    weed truths of the cranks and outcasts
                    like ourselves.
If they work,
they fit. If they don't,
they fail. This is not
                    just evolution, not
fitness as the root of all being
                              at the expensive
                              gore of others.
What works allows
for the whole range of the possible,
the full
interaction
                    with the way things are
                    with no
                    sadness,
                              especially for you
with your lethal pains,
your stalled,
still water depressions
in history's boiling sun.
You could row a galleon
                    single-handed with your mind.
You warned against
"a premature closing
of our accounts
with reality," of not
going far enough,

or trusting deep enough
that the Mystery
is more than we can exhaust,
like the fruits of "methodical self-suggestion,"
telling yourself
who you want yourself to be,
adding desire
to reality, shaping you
into who you really are.
Your heart was unshaken
in the "game of human life."
Your self-rescue,
self-creation,
your garden of affirming habits,
brought you to the point
where you could weed away
the despair of your times, and actually
"stand
the universe."
Why does the Mystery respond to us?
We know it must.
It does.
Faith, philosophy,
all the holy nows,
are the inward fields
of everyone's life, the great rapids
of consciousness and
conscience,
the fecund ponds of
neurosis,
the underground caverns,
the sinks

of thought
turning up miles later
in the springs of calm beginnings.
                              It's the same
                              for all of us, though

different folk "find their minds
more at home in very different
fragments of the world."

When you walked with Freud to the train, you had to pause
to let angina pass, telling Freud to walk on, and he did
in admiration of your stride slowly catching up behind him.
He knew you had already led the way, more at home
than he had ever been
with death's
rank plurality.

In Palo Alto, in the San Francisco quake,
your rooms swaying around you, your body was terrified, but you
were exulting in the power of the world wobbling
reality to the quick.
                    Vitality overrides.
                    It supersedes.
                    It is the force behind
the logos. No one "lives
in external truth, among the salts and acids,
but in the warm phantasmagoric chamber of his brain
with the painted windows and the storied walls."
All facts are guesses,
even the dogma of the gods.
                        "Fallibilism" you coined it,
sounds like a Roman orgy cult,

the inner fallible quivering,
                              but it's only
                              the universal
                              redemption
of limitation—to be the truth, despite
                                        not being enough.
                                        "The whole preferred."
Good or bad, god or devil,
the "or"
            always excludes. It "keeps us
            as foreigners
                        in relation to god."
Monism,
all the Only Good Gods,
                        has its nasty, invasive
ethical aliens
seeping across
theological borders
                    —no profiling possible.
                    They look like all of us.
But you knew
the unstoppable
possible
shows us we are free
                    to change our thoughts
so our inner selves
can heal
        "the outer aspects" of our lives.
Over and over
you said it,
            seeking the most
            freedom for all.

"Philosophies
are intimate parts
of the universe,
they express something of its own
thought of itself."
E pluribus unum.
                    One can't have it
                    if all don't have it.

A hundred years before the universe was called
a multiverse,
                    you understood the plural All,
                    all at once,
                    everywhere, equal
                    but not the same
                    anywhere, all the time, including
the innerverse
of each of us
where the ayes have it or they don't,
where every choice, all Catch-22s, are settled
if only we
                    "unclamp" and open ourselves
                    to the prudent
                    positive with news
from a good scout like you who tells us,
                              ¦   from his own dilemmas

that "to miss the joy
is to miss all."

NOTE: William James died in 1910 at the age of sixty-eight from heart failure after suffering for years from acute angina. He met Freud and Jung at a conference at Clark University in Worchester, Massachusetts, almost a year before his death. His great works, *The Principles of Psychology* (1890) and *The Varieties of Religious Experience* (1900), as well as *Pragmatism* (1907) and *A Pluralistic Universe* (1909), along with his technique of "methodical self-suggestion," helped set the stage for applied psychology and opened the door for alternative forms of healing in the United States and even, I believe, creating an American receptiveness to Viktor Frankl's logo therapy and psychiatric stoicism. James knew that mind didn't create reality alone, it collaborated with objective fact though the mechanism of personal experience. He knew that interpretation could kill, ennoble, save, or deprive. And he sought to understand what thoughts worked when it came to securing health and sanity.

James, as a healer, believed it was up to us as individuals to create systems and ideas that are "friendly and genial" to human betterment, a task to which he devoted his life as a person and as a cultural mentor.

The Wanderers: H.D. (1886–1961)

Give me language, sure Muses, to say this mind
that could see the inner world on the stage of time,
the legends of ourselves, heroic outside in,
spread on long clean pages, pared to nothing less,
a proscenium of poems opening to hope.

It is her mind, not
some standard mind,

not a mind by rote,
but hers "buried alive,"

an Antigone,
knowing the good,

against all absolutes,
all tyrannies insisting

on the moral form,
the letter, even when

it tortured the spirit
to give up in boredom

the coffin of gossip
and defy the living death

of those alive
with no life of their own.

It is her mind
that dreamed itself back

alive from the dregs
of duty, glass crypts,

knowing one's place
in the hideous

impiety of violence,
two world wars,

the vivisection
of millions.

Love tricked
into torment,

it was her mind
and way of being who she is,

her mind that moved
the constellations closer

to sincerity, her mind caught
in the trenches and the blitz

like a leg
in a shark's maw,

Thanatos
in his black mask

conspicuous among the chorus
of premature angels,

dark Eros singing
through phobic vistas,

the broken bookstores
and cathedrals,

echo chamber
concert halls,

mazes of the shattered
and the rendered,

her mind
called to the real

in the lost forests
of these columns

and sacred groves
behind the eyes,

written
in inner hieroglyphs,

the palimpsest
of misogyny and battle,

brother killed,
father broken

unto death
by death,

husband
brain spasmed

by trench rats,
death's head

machine guns, gas.
And in the bombing,

she learned to liberate
herself in the present

by becoming her own myth,
a sphinx of maps and quests

riddling its freedom from the codes
of metaphor emerging

to unbolt experience
from the threat of cruelty,

sadism, feudal sex wars,
women chained like ocean waves

caught in iron vats so vast
even the sky can't see the walls.

It is her mind
that is the island

of solace,
her *Tribute to Freud*

that was a free
association, both of them

approaching Hitler's rack,
conversing kindly through the groans

while the end of the world
chalked swastikas

on sidewalks
so no Jew would ever be

passed over again.
Her mind, not

some robot mind,
her mind shows

how adaptation works,
how evolution flows by choice

when we move through
an opening in chance,

even with a wrong
theory to lead the way,

a map with so much right,
while the content was

ridiculously wrong.
But all luck is an opening.

No flaws matter
that are true mistakes.

Freud was a porter
through the jungle.

He knew where the lost
treasures lay, the lost valley

high in spiritual longing,
the actuality of hope that can't

be overridden
by reality and its "facts."

She was always true
to her own orbit, "firm

in her own small,
static, limited" sphere

so that "living within,"
she begot "self-out-of-self,

selfless that pearl
of great price," the grace

of being, the opus
that never ran dry.

She lived a mind
that wouldn't cut and run,

Blitz Wanderer,
Freud Spelunker.

The exact
enthralled her.

The in-
competent word

never dared her.
She polished her mind

until she could see
clean through the soul

of the sad mystery
play of the past,

the epic
of the Self,

Psyche reborn
through the shattered world,

H.D. digging in,
telling herself truth

beyond the truth.
Hilda, Helen, Hellas,

Mother Helen,
"powerful, powerless,

all powerful,"
Helen's problem: to be

dismissed by her own
fated beauty, the irresistible

curve of lip, the posture
of erotic poise,

a collected, acquired,
stolen thing to be had

with no being beneath
the divine reflection:

Misogyny's flawless trick
to glorify the surface

and deny the core.
But the "object"

had her own
desires.

With the only life
she had, she undermined

the patriarchal farce,
father's Trojan horse,

the one plus one
is two, a nuclear

implosion, her
in her family

a nut between
two stones:

Father vacuum,
Mother void.

Sexism lays a nest
for racism

and dominion over all:
Misogyny, the first

crime against
humanity.

She would sanction
none of it, ever,

never, always she was
her own clean way.

Her love
life a map

of how the future
devours

the chains
of the past

without ever
smacking its lips.

She just was
as she had to be.

"The fact
of writing

is the thing
—it trains one"

"to a sort of yogic
magic power,"

"it is a sort
of contemplation,

it is living
on another plane,

it is 'traveling in the astral'...
that is the thing."

The alchemy
of practice

is the lens
to examine

the whole culture,
all of civilization,

as it lives in us,
changes through our genes

and habits;
we are what has happened to it;

it breaks down in us,
just as it rides us into the ground

with its errors
and its hates

until we refuse it,
like refusing to rot inside.

It was the "dragon"
of "war terror" in her

that gives her to us now
with no sentiment for progress;

she knew politics
shreds flesh.

As the bombs and doodlebugs fell
on London's green grocers, theaters,

neighborhood pubs, the sleepless horrors
of hospitals, undergrounds, morgues,

she did salvage work
up and down,

pulling sanity
from debris while she

refused to leave,
refused to be driven out

by mere terrors.
Freud, the ironic

honest papa,
gave her a golden bough

when she was through;
"the boughs... are twisted

by many bafflings";
that small orange tree branch

gave her the key
to go beyond him

to see war, the dragon,
as the patriarch's

snarling
dementia,

the family curse
"of man" that saturates

all that stands, even when
the walls do not fall.

Freud, the Sybil,
"set me free

to prophesy," to "... dare, seek,
seek further, dare more."

The blitz "goes
a step further

toward the fine
distillation of emotion,

the elixir of life,
the philosopher's stone

is yours if you surrender
sterile logic, trivial reason;

so mind dispersed, dared occult lore,
found secret doors unlocked..."

"Let us substitute
enchantment for sentiment,

re-dedicate our gifts
to spiritual realism..."

Helen's myth
was damned,

exiled
in a doomed city,

but she herself
was free

in Vienna,
London, Luxor,

where Paris is
a chronic form,

a lure
to insignificance,

Paris,
that spark, that

impertinence, that
partialness,

so inadequate,
so seductive

as lesser
child men are, so far

beyond dear,
dread Aphrodite's

sacred pale.
H.D. like Helen

frozen for a moment
in a style, a fated reputation,

she out-wrote, out-lived, survived
in sanity the pig male sculptor

who squawked best in Pisa
received a short oblivion

in St. Elizabeth's
dirty bath.

Helen doomed,
Hermes delivered:

H.D. a Hermetic
Definition,

a life of sublime
interpretation,

the secret life of all
who make new things,

a seismograph of the most
intimate distances

and emotional furrows
of the wars blooming

into corpses, or lives lost
in the rubble of themselves.

Ancient wisdom
sees the universe

as a code
from which all

that is holy
is divined; chance

encounters morphed
into legends,

Rafer Johnson
is Olympia,

Orphic symbols
and Freudian mazes,

linking tribal myths
to personal dreams,

Orpheus in Helen mask,
a muse disguised

as Sigmund's flat.
The palimpsest:

Moravian women,
divine

in their purpose
and perfection.

Phony Pound,
faking till

he made it;
the Spanish Flu,

Perdita, Bryher,
Love's saving grace,

seance chats
with teenage pilots

downed and dead,
that alchemy of the damaged

soul into a good life saved
that led to the Professor

and his empowering
need to be loved;

community and capitalism
crashing in on each other;

then the after-Blitz
breakdown, and then

like a final, boring
horror of "the bomb,"

all along
kept alive

by Helen
as alter ego;

end days
a captive

of recuperation,
a caged owl like Ezra

the palimpsest,
written, overwritten

all life long.
And her, Athena's

wisest darling. "But I
went on, I had to go on.

The writing was the unborn
the conception..."

"... write, write or die."
Aphrodite's wonders,

Her snares, Her traps,
Her mazes,

the false steps
—Her lesson

is to trust
love, trust Her

when She
is in love

with you
enough

to give you
the mystery

of Her love
to surrender to.

Her way was to go and see
what hadn't been seen,

to make sense of maps
that hadn't been drawn,

to find the sources
of coming alive,

of self-resurrection,
like being tossed twice

in a tornado, just missed
by all the broken glass,

auto parts and tractors,
a helpless cat in history,

but one with a mind
that turned hell into myth

and myth into sanity.
Buried alive

in our lives,
we all need guides

to find our way out
into the life

that wants us to be;
"write, write or die,"

that is the guide,
simplify the language,

grasp the patterns
in unbearable

complexity,
make a world

to live in that
you can understand.

"Nike seemed to be
my own especial sign,

or part of
my hieroglyph."

What we know
in our depths

comes always
as a gift we cause

by trusting openness
to take it in,

like chance has
given Sappho's

shattered line
a perfect breath

from patchwork scraps,
mummy stuffings, scholastic

citings of the Tenth
Muse's ruined leavings,

so fragments are
cuplets, salvaged

crumbs of words
that showed a whole

generation how to write.
So she, H.D.,

Sappho's daughter,
comrade, Hermes born,

healing thief of tombs
and dungeons, says

on her grave stone that
"Greek ecstasy reclaims forever

one who died
following intricate song's

lost measure," words true
one upon another,

dense, clear,
so complex

that thinking
makes it so,

woven time
mind's palimpsest,

Penelope's trick
dodging terrible

necessity, her decisive
indecision, day after day,

was her
inner victory

and Athena's mirth
at big boy bluster,

those flaccid elders
who claim God's ear,

who are as ludicrous as
the absent phallus is

proof of lost endowment,
as funny as the cosmos is sincere.

NOTE: Hilda Doolittle (H.D.), classicist and modernist, refused to be chattel, refused to be smothered in Victorian patriarchal dross. Some have tried to dismiss her by defining her through her associations with D. H. Lawrence, Ezra Pound, Sigmund Freud, and William Carlos Williams, dismissed in much the same way that Lou Andreas-Salomé is dismissed as a writer by her associations with Nietzsche, Rilke, and Freud. Both women suffer from the demeaning shadows of celebrity culture. H.D.'s greatness is in her genius for universalizing personal narratives and finding their symbolic place in the broader mythic cycles that underlie the spiritual perspectives of the twentieth century.

The Warriors: Rachel Carson (1907–1964)

Guide me, stern muses, to a voice that can say
this life of outrage and of duty's honor,
this generous life that gave its health away
to tell unwelcome truths and show
what no one wants to see, the secret welts and bruises
of crude, manslaughtering abuse.

It has come to this, so far—
that nothing she saw and suffered, nothing

has changed in sixty years—nothing
and in a time when everything else has changed,

from linotypes to laptops,
the Cold War, the Soviet collapse,

podcasts, cellphones, the nano juggling of atoms—
only the belittling, the sour lying,

the arrogant scorn, the supercilious
claims of expert hirelings,

only these sinkholes in conscience
have stayed the same, covering up

a lethal and lecherous neglect
so profit preachers in powder blue suits

will never perp walk, puke with guilt, pay up.
An agent of reality, of which most of us

"cannot bear very much," Rachel Carson
witnessed the execution-gas invisibility,

the fatal fog of fortune-making
subsidized by zero-cost pollution,

pick-pocket lobbyists lifting tax breaks:
"The perfume of those pesticides

is the scent of freedom.
Let the market ring."

But Carson, dignified, patriotic,
loyal to the land, she served the true

uncertainty of science in the savage first
skirmishes with those for whom

everything could be sacrificed
to a single end, and any means to get there, even

cancer profits, moth-eaten, mad
growth ideology fueled by a criminal

fleecing of the poor-to-do, conning them
to think they could afford what they could not

pay for, endless growth, the unstoppable
delusion, writing off the future

health of children, like a bad speculation,
and the lives of anyone too frail financially to fight back.

These were the covert addicts
of the vice of wealth she fought,

the fixers who buy off science tricksters
to dope up data into decoy facts,

distracting us with doubts to cover up
the money lechery of their intent.

And she could see their scam coming,
like gypsies swarming and feasting on rubes,

making propaganda seem like the noble
uncertainty of science shilling for the "truth."

Doubt the searchers, who doubt themselves,
serving reality, free of everything but data,

counter them with bribed savants
who serve and cannot doubt a lying master.

More, More, More, the Sin of More
bulging with wasted plenty, dosing us

with careless malice one by one while we
hand over our heads and wallets

to conveyor-belt whitecoats as if
they were faith healers feasting on patients

then drooling for treats. Even she
couldn't face it at first.

"Some of the thoughts... were so unattractive...
I rejected them completely.... It was pleasant to believe...

that much of Nature was forever beyond
the tampering reach of man." To have such thoughts

"even vaguely threatened was so shocking
that I shut my mind—refused to acknowledge

what I couldn't help seeing." What she saw
seemed impossible, a sleight of mind: whole businesses,

gentlemen of good standing, willfully, secretly,
turning the land they live on into a toilet that spews

shit into the lungs of their own children,
using the land up like a slave as if it were worthless

without being used, exhausted
without a cost, the whole earth

a frayed old rug to sweep
crimes under until it gets

so bumpy the dog trips
and falls into the cat who leaps

and knocks over the lamp
that hits you on the knee

and sends you reeling into a wall
for a fatal concussion. Absurd as it is,

as making money off killing yourself,
you and your chances are still

dead as doornails. Killing bugs
that eat profits with stuff that can kill

everything around it, including you,
if you have the right cocktail of genes

and history, is like smoking, like building
bombs so big they require whole cities of the sick

to make them, to make tens of thousands of them
when five or ten of them could ruin the world

as we know it, and all of us in it,
good genes or not.

Carson couldn't be scammed.
She knew that everything

is connected to everything else;
that everything has to go somewhere,

that you can't orphan the land without
it coming back to take you down

like starving wolves catch the sleigh
and ravage you and your exhausted horses.

It took all her genius for truth
to believe her own eyes:

that it was possible
to commit suicide

without knowing it,
using the laughing gas

of terminal mass stupidity,
suckling on a death-psychosis economy

that righteously debunks humility,
and caution, as bad for business,

that's it's possible for us to butcher ourselves
with tools we can't control, cutting off our own

limbs with chainsaws that break
our shoulder joints and fall

ripping through a thigh or shin.
Who could believe it? Who could believe

that martini men, Sunday sluggers,
barbecue masters, Little League dads,

did what they were told, dumped
poison where kids could get at it

just to keep their jobs
and feed their own.

No, no, no, they were told,
there's ample room for doubt

that if you pull the pin and release the handle
the grenade won't explode.

Everyone knows that. Just keep the thing
in a drawer, the kids won't find it.

These dark blisterings of hubris
are so farcical, even the touchy gods

are embarrassed and turn away.
Not Rachel Carson. Such monstrosities

were for her a natural history
to be defined, the quest of a lifetime,

important enough for her to risk
being in public who she was in the farthest

most private part of herself, fearless
in the face of abhorred anomalies,

schoolmarm steady, rock salt of the earth,
old fashioned as spine, stern,

decent, never one to abandon
the troubles that needed her heart.

She was called to the good and the true.
She couldn't refuse. And she didn't.

They gave her a life to be proud of
as the stress of honor

helped the cancer polish her off,
her life a storm full of enemies,

like aphid squalls on roses, chewing on
anyone more concerned with health

than wealth, turning her into
a doily of misogyny, an hysteric prude,

a sweet old dingbat dealing in false fear,
pushing caution like a drug.

Does it sound novelistic to say that? It's not.
Polluters really don't care. That's the ultimate

shock, the wild reality. Business
is a team sport. Take no prisoners, win,

no flinching, never lose
or you're lost. The paycheck,

steak on the table, breadwinner pride,
us against them, these easily

justify any means. And besides,
no one, of course, except an actual fiend,

thinks they're doing anyone harm.
Chlorinated hydrocarbons, like the miracle

of DDT, dichloro-diphenyl-trichloro-ethane,
that kills enemy germs, while killing

their victims like a sniper at long range
that no one can see. Same for chlordane,

heptachlor, dioxin, dieldrin, aldrin,
endrin, nerve gases used to kill bugs

and trench-trapped soldiers,
parathion, malathion, and a cosmos more,

including radionuclids plentiful as cannibal beetles,
and in all doses, all at once, or in as many

breaths as one takes in a decade, deadly as venom.
"We make jobs. We put food on your table.

Our business is based on science for better living.
How can we do wrong? We're innocent

until proven guilty. We know we're not bad,
so nothing bad will probably happen.

You'll have to prove your slander
beyond a reasonable doubt.

We doubt harm and danger.
That's enough to acquit us."

(Just as probable cause
is enough to indict.)

But there's no crime until
something terrible happens

"beyond our control."
It's all a muddle of intent.

No one wants to assume evil.
But we are left with suspicions

of callousness, inattention, indifference.
But malice aforethought?

A conspiracy to make money
by killing off consumers

when they're finally too old any more
to consume? Not beyond the realm

of the spreadsheet, the quarterly report
and actuarial, though without, of course

direct intent? Oh, come on.
Not giving a hoot

is a moral sin of omission.
But like the great wanderer,

Carson was true
to her orbit too.

Her standards
were a gamble

not worth the risk
of not taking.

She spoke the evidence, saw
cancer's tracks, amazing

as a leopard's stalking us
idle in our harmless sloth and sloppiness,

its tracks all around us
while we cheat and feign,

hiding our poisoned socks
under the bed.

She would gather what strength she could
from radiation knowing full well

that what killed the cancer
could kill her, and was surely a cousin

of what caused her body such pain,
though never mentioning its obvious source.

And if she had referenced her health,
they'd have used it against her,

accused her of using the cancer card
like a girlie trick to pull pity.

She would have burned off her hand
before doing something like that,

so Roman, so Stoic she turned out to be.
She knew that when "that intangible

cycle had run its course,
it was natural and no unhappy thing

that a life comes to an end."
To think otherwise would be

a final folly of "man against
himself" and the order of the way it is.

Everything dies, soft or hard, early or on time.
Some go like wiping the countertop of dust,

whole species mopped up; some go tortured, some
die in the bed they were born in. Rachel Carson

felt the cancer in her bones every step she took;
she did not want to cause pain or premature

annihilation for anything, even indirectly.
"It is time that human beings admit

their kinship
with other forms of life."

You don't harm your relatives, unless
you're a sociopath. Making whales go deaf

from sonar just wouldn't happen if
we knew who we really are, flesh and blood

kin with all life in the world. It's really
no different than giving a baby

boiling water to stop it crying without
knowing what the water will do, or why

it's hot—this making of things
and using them without

calculating risk, paving the way
through carelessness

so a new technique
is "embedded in a vast

economic and political
commitment" almost as impossible

to stop as compound interest,
as a train roaring full bore

through a sleepy town.
We live in "a sea of carcinogens."

Rather than stop the way
of life that made them,

and rebuild a world we can bear,
we choose to try to cure

the cancers we've loosed upon us.
And why not prevention

over cure?
We all know why.

She knew why
as she was dying

and being ridiculed
by her proxy killers.

Even wonder can't
snooker the lust for profit.

You can't stop money
from making money,

until it can make
as much or more

another way. And that's
why the big curtain

has come undone
and dropped on the stage

way before the end
was meant to commence,

the house going dark
and time running out

before being over,
the circle of health

an open wound
pumping out life

like a pool of blood
in a spotlight,

with all eyes blank,
opaque cloudy stare.

NOTE: Rachel Carson died of a heart attack in 1964 some two years after the publication of *Silent Spring*, at age fifty-four. Weakened by radiotherapy, the cancer spreading to her pelvis and spleen, suffering from anemia and pneumonia, she continued to give witness to the literally unbelievable madness she saw so clearly until weeks before she died.

The Warriors: John Aaron Lewis (1920–2001)
"Afternoon in Paris": 1957

It's a hundred and one and melting in your old hometown, John.
Tomatoes are wilting, basil's dead, we sweat monsoons,
the doctor's lost his mind to death,
and you're long gone, but not your vibe.

I wish our cops had some; they'd stop exploding
the bodies of crazy folks and drunks
with electrocution wands and firefight bullets
with no one firing back, here in Albuquerque

where you lost your mother in the 1920s, your world at four
falling apart, raised up again by grandma and great granny,
taught piano by an auntie in a house around Broadway
        south of Central
where a theater one day is named for you,

in Albuquerque, where you played piano in a Boy Scout band,
earned fifty cents a Sunday playing to the choir, a budding ethno-
musicologist of the bars who cooled everyone down on First Street
and at UNM, a student of music and culture

before going to war in '42, ten years before the MJQ
        revved up,
the Banana King Market still on Central run by the man
        with coke-bottle glasses,
green frogs lounging in the mud along the ditches,
        barking as they jump
with their syncopated plop, bebop, Bach and blues
        cooling through the willows,

an acequia vibe smooth as time.
We're all here at the Outpost, John,
meditating jazz time into verse time,
        nothing as cool as you, though,
as your classical mind, its imperturbable riffs,

your calm breezy smile, eyebrows rising right on key,
such passionate restraint, such purposeful abandonment.
We're all here, and we're not half as cool as you
        but I only speak for myself,
of course. But we're trying.

How about a Parisian lemonade? Ice cream sundae clouds
        along the Seine,
Count Basie not far away. A stroll up the Champs-Élysées
and across the river to Eiffel's wonder
where Hitler stomped and smirked his Wagnerian contempt

and the world fell apart again, and kept on falling,
just couldn't stop, cold wars too hot to hold, no peace, no please
just insight from the keys years later. "Afternoon in Paris"
        played and recorded
in Paris 1957, thirteen years from the last Sieg Heil
        in the Deux Magots

when the world still needed the iceberg-cool blues
        of your piano unruffled, un-riled.
Dark vibes still staining Sorbonne's walls
        where resistance partisans were glad
to be shot and bled not strangled with a rope from a Metro
        art nouveau.
1957, French Foreign Legionnaires on every Left Bank corner,

Tommy guns poised, fingers tense for Algerians with Freedom
    in their spines
to fall from the skies, to blast them into the fog
    and accordion snooze cheesy blue
cigarette smoke when they came to reap revenge
    for torture, occupation,
decades of French bad breath. The Black and White Club
    off the Boule-Miche,

beautiful people safe for while in a dungeon world. Gin and jazz,
blue black body heat, far from Pasternak in the Soviet Cold
    who smacked a hole
in the iron curtain, Zhivago smuggled out, published in Paris
    by an outlawed
Italian communist, who else, in 1957 just when you
    and the Quartet

were playing away the tears of decades. 1957, Toscanini dies,
    Elvis on Ed Sullivan
for the last time, waist-up only. 1957, Camus wins the Nobel Prize
and feels like a sellout with a target on his back,
    the Modern Jazz Quartet
proves smoother than Wild Turkey on the rocks
    spiked with twilight;

and Whamo Corp. promotes a rage for Frisbees, Bogart dies;
the KKK makes Willie Edwards jump off a bridge
into the Alabama River where he drowns. Jim Crow dangling
by his broken soul and Little Rock sneering, growling
    at a beautiful child

too wise and cool to show her fear on the way to a better school.
     And you, John,
wiser than the wise, upright, vital as ever, seeing jazz grown
     from plantation horrors
as part of Bach's evolving sound and Bach a part of yours.
1957, "Howl," blasting from an English page, is seized
     by customs goons at Ellis Island

for being obscene. 1957 John Lewis, Sasha Distel,
     Barney Wilen, Persey Heath,
Pierre Michelot, Kenny Clarke, Connie Kay,
     no Milt Jackson yet,
syncopate Paris in the shade, while across the great Atlantic
and west of the Llano Estacado, southeast of South Broadway,
     a forty-two-thousand-pound

hydrogen bomb falls from a B-29 near the Sunport, unarmed,
     but leaving a crater
circled with spikes of plutonium and other monsters
     of the periodic table.
While John's in Paris composing to heal the world,
     Strom Thurmond filibuster gasses for twenty-four hours
to stop the Civil Rights Act dead in its tracks, and fails.

And Kerouac *On the Road* goes on sale,
     Sputnik I becomes Uncle Sam's
dazed blush, and the high thin strato sky's first chuck
     of litter, the first of millions
and space debris was stillborn like a Hydra's many heads
     from death.
1957, Gabriela Mistral, Joe McCarthy, Jean Sibelius,

Christian Dior meet each other on death's third rail.
And all the while they're dancing to the MJQ
        on Saint-Germain-des-Prés,
on the tables at the Café de Flore, Sartre and Beauvoir might
        even have seen you play
on purpose, perhaps, Americans still oddities to the French,
        your smile

softening even existential guile, and they damn well knew it.
And all I'm left with are choppy words, of course, while you
        still make the stars
skip and roll in fugues and riffs of counterpoint and poise,
        a classical precision,
improv with a purpose. "How High the Sputnik" replaced
        by "Dear Old Stockholm"

as jazz anthem for the ages. "Afternoon in Paris" proceeding
like kids skipping rope, playing jacks, racing through
        fire-hydrant rain,
doing the soft shoe all the way home for fun, all free and released
by the liberty of order in the notes from John Lewis's mind
        and fingers

so the world had joy to take more seriously for a moment
        than all the hells of
Algeria or Korea not long before. 1957. "All the Things You
        Are" so solo supreme,
sublime, brushing the drums of the world's heart, "I Cover
        the Waterfront,"
"Bags Groove," "Willow Weep for Me"; mighty is this cool,
        grateful is the fool

too happy to be fooled as the world falls apart again
     and keeps on falling
and coming apart. It just can't stop, too hot,
no peace in sight, no please, just insight from the keys
from the CD in my hot car in Albuquerque June

as cool conquers all, and the wise man with the calming smile
     I feel
with piano sound from starched cuffs sweet and crisp in my ear
cures all fools like me of fear. This cool conquering is all,
too smooth to be fooled by mere ideas of gloom-to-be because

John knew the world keeps falling apart
and mending its tune,
and coming unglued
and mending its tune. John knew.

NOTE: Born in Albuquerque on March 29, 1920, the pianist and
composer John Lewis was the founder and director of the Modern
Jazz Quartet. Trained in anthropology at the University of New
Mexico, Lewis joined Dizzy Gillespie's bop-style big band in New
York. Associated with jazz greats such as Miles Davis, Charlie
Parker, Duke Ellington, Count Basie, Lester Young, and Ella
Fitzgerald, Lewis also performed fugues of J. S. Bach, composed the
masterpiece "Afternoon in Paris," and was at home with both the
blues and the work of Igor Stravinsky. For me, Lewis is a warrior
Homeric American because he battled the stereotypes of race and
musical tradition to be supremely his own person, following his own
inclinations despite whatever obstacles he encountered.

from

Museum Poems
(2011–2018)

Bloody Hell
Rini Price (1941–2019)
Acrylic on canvas, 40" x 30", 2008
Albuquerque Museum of Art and History,
permanent collection

It's what showed up.
Nothing in it

was pre-determined,
except to do it in the world

as it is; Grace by any other name
would be as clean, decade after decade.

When we're present and prepared
the truth can appear through us

like "Bloody Hell" one day, a gory fury
at idiot brutality, a Pantocrater erupting

in poised berserker rage, an axe wielding
wisdom, icon of a time when tolerance

is a cop-out and anger itself
incompetent and deadening in the face

of intolerable foolery and terror.
"Bloody Hell" knows the arrogant bunglers,

the hyena cruel, the rapacious dunces, mindless
in their certainty, and comes alive as an indictment

of mind-fuck piranhas, the political tortures of the times,
the rationalized raping of the world, of land,

of children, women and men, of hope, of reason,
of compassion, of simple sanity, screaming bloody hell

and wielding havoc, tornadoes of deeds,
of meat-red rage flaying open the catastrophe

of those who force all others to be less
than who they are, or could be,

showing skinned the dismissers, the deniers
who give nothing, not even a first chance,

thousands upon thousands of generations buried alive
by ricos, gatekeepers, corporate seducers, insane

tyrants who thrive on the ghost lives
of those who toil, dignified, hungry,

too good to hate to their bones
those who work them raw, dissolve them

into wealth they never see,
make them compost for idle beauties,

then cower, blame and lie
when bloody hell boils over—all over them.

NOTE: "Bloody Hell" was painted shortly before the presidential
election of 2008 after eight years of the George W. Bush
administration. "It was painted not so much with political intent
as it was a response to the election. It was the way I was feeling
about the political world at the time," said Rini Price.

Approaching Storm, Pueblo Alto, Chaco Canyon, New Mexico
Kirk Gittings (b. 1950)
Black and white photograph, 1982
The Meadows Museum, Hermetic Collections,
The Great Hall

Lightning strikes have left in death
bodies of teachers and hikers in our lifetimes there.
We've missed the hit several times ourselves

in that place where nothing can go wrong,
where lightning's luck, where no false steps can happen,
no tragedies, no accidents, no truths beyond

what comes to be in a place so powerful
it fills up doubt, fills up fear, fills up
suspicion and even the cynical

demons at work in reason, fills them up
like sand in crevasses, leaves the landscape of the mind
steady as geology is, most of the time.

It is oracular and jubilant to be there
self-making in the ruins from which
the future unfolds in psychic space so real

perfection strikes right over it,
so white, so loud, so free of all
possible constraint, it appears

in the space of your eye, a blink of lightning
like traces of grace in mishaps never come to life.
We have been to Alto, climbed the cliffs, chased down

by thunderheads darker than philosophy,
sure-brained for anything, on snow that makes the lichen
slick as ice, and have survived our chances

to become the future within us; nothing
gets in the way of what will be, though a single
lightening in the mind, one thought, can change it.

NOTE: Kirk Gittings took this photograph during his multiple trips
to Chaco Canyon to make the award-winning photographs for *Chaco
Body*, our collaboration published by Artspace Press in 1991. This
image was one of a dozen negatives he took with his wooden and
brash 4" x 5" Japanese view camera made by Tachihara. Two of the
dozen images had lightning strikes, but only one was over Pueblo
Alto atop Chacra Mesa north of Pueblo Bonito. The storm eventually
hit and "blew down on me," Gittings said. He made the mistake of
trying to avoid the lightning by going down an arroyo, which almost
immediately flash flooded with boulders crashing down. Luckily he
was on a little ledge above the water. Once the storm passed, the
day "was glorious," he said, and he had one of the iconic images of
American archaeological photography.

Angel Teaching a Dog
the Rudiments of Flight
Rini Price (1941–2019)
Acrylic on canvas, 36" x 30", 1993–1994
The Meadows Museum, Hermetic Collections,
The Old Great Room

If liftoff is achieved
by unconditional joy,
and angels are airborne

from the purest pleasure
in being angels, the dog
who would, like us,

aspire to such heights,
she's been flying,
with her inner puppy all awing,

since the Angel first
feathered up to be
lighthearted as Her pupil

overjoying gravity
like the boundless dog transcends
all fours and fur, watching

the greater She who flies on
with celestial calm
knowing that all is

exactly as it must be, always:
She can't doubt it
because She is it, as an angel,

and joy without doubt
gives wings to everything,
even rocks and trees

like Orpheus does
singing through the clouds.
And the dog of great expectations,

with her conductor's tail,
needs no wings to soar
with carefree wonder

at being without care.
The Angel knew
her protegè from afar,

spotting her wagging around
street-happy kids—it does,
it takes one to know one.

In the free heart of the world
what is will soar, as it is
—even dogs, even us—

when joy cuts loose
its clinging doubt,
and the ballast

of genes and sad reason
turns to blowing sand below
the gentle glee of letting go.

NOTE: This painting is from our *Death Self* collaborative series. It is paired with my poem "Death Is the Rest." A *Death Self* exhibition of paintings and poems took place at Artspace 116 in Albuquerque from March through May of 2005. A catalogue of the exhibition, with color reproductions of the paintings in company with the poems, was published in 2005 by Wingspread Guides of New Mexico, Inc.

Judith Slaying Holofernes
Artemisia Gentileschi (1593–1652)
Oil on canvas, 199 cm x 1162 cm, circa 1614–1620
Galleria degli Uffizi, Florence, Italy

The thumbscrew was
a double screw, first
the rapist then
the father suing
the rapist for your
lost virginity and his
lost formulas for paint,
the court then
torturing you
to get the truth
you'd already given
only to find
you were truer in your honor
than all the actual pain
of their horrific insult.
And you, then, Artemisia,
turned them all into stags
devoured by dogs gnawing on history,
nameless gristle replacing fame
—rapist and father,
and court and church,
all oppressors, all
idiots of dark matter sadism, all
swagger-bully
potbellied blowfish-stinking no-minds, all
shadowed by your genius,
and the head
of Holofernes,
of all tyrannical authority,

swinging along
as you walk away
from the sword
and the sawing,
the drunken head
in the bag.

NOTE: Artemisia Gentileschi began this painting in 1612, one year after the publication in England of The King James version of the Bible and Shakespeare's *The Tempest*. In 1612 she was also tortured with thumbscrews to ensure her veracity, as was the custom, when she testified in a trial against Agostino Tassi, a man accused by her father of raping her. A friend of Galileo and admired by Michelangelo, Gentileschi's painting of heroic Judith cutting off the head of the conquering oppressor Holofernes is the most famous image of that moment in biblical history when a woman does what no man could do.

The Sleep of Reason Produces Monsters
Francisco de Goya (1746–1828)
Etching, ink on paper, Plate 43, 21.5 cm x 15 cm, circa 1797–1799
Viewed at the Albuquerque Museum, March 2012

It's not sleeping reason
that lets the monsters through the gates,

it's when reason buries itself
awake in subterranean truths

behind all civility, all
rationality, so that logic

dresses up as gentlemen
tormentors and rises up

through grids and graphs
like giant rats in satin capes

and bustles, parading
through dining rooms of oligarchs

where crumbs are simply
not enough anymore,

where shoes and even
feet are meat for paradise

among the monsters who sing and munch
without the false fronts

and trapdoors of mentation.
There below the surface, old

guillotines rust along
with rotting gibbets and garrote

posts, flowing scarves
caught in spokes, strangling

a nation of graceful political
seducers half exposed in slogans

and titilations of power
jerking and dancing

at the groaning reason is
not made to comprehend.

NOTE: Los Caprichos are a suite of eighty aquatints created by
Francisco Goya in 1797–98. In Goya's words, they depict "the
innumerable foibles and follies to be found in any civilized society,
and from the common prejudices and deceitful practices which
custom, ignorance or self-interest have made usual." The bats and
devil owls that plague the sleeping Goya in this image were the devils
the Enlightenment tried to banish; it succeeded in America, for the
briefest of moments, when the Bill of Rights was ratified in 1791.

Description IS Second Nature
Allan Graham/Toadhouse (1943–2019)
Color ink and graphite on canvas, 50" x 38", circa 2015
Personal collection

Seven billion
second natures,
seven billion
seven billion
stories,
seven billion
as IS-es,
more,
far more,
infinitely
more description
than
the poor corpse
described.

NOTE: The American painter, poet, and visual humorist Allan "Skip" Graham, aka Toadhouse, lived and worked with his wife, the artist Gloria Graham, in an off-the-grid strawbale house with studios on the edge of the Pecos Wilderness near San Jose, New Mexico. Graham's versatility including making punning fine art bumper stickers and placing them on chromed bumpers that gallery visitors viewed as they might in an uncanny parking lot. *Description IS Second Nature* states his fundamental principle of direct, unfiltered experience, both verbally and visually, and represents a moment in his adventure with the comic and sublime. A richly productive poet and visual artist, his work is on display in public and private collections around the world. Graham died of a heart ailment at seventy-two in January 2019.

Map #2 (from Personal Cartography)
Barbara Byers (b. 1952)
Confused media on paper—bleach, string, ink,
    and colored papers, 27" x 20", circa 2014
Personal collection

Star cluster,
on paper,
without
burning holes
in the blue
of the deep
cosmic
comic
at work
through the genes
in jeans,
unbleached,
the universe
so many Levis
shrunk to the leg
in the bath tub,
fitting us
like a second skin
once we think it
past thought
and make something
of it.

NOTE: American painter and builder of objects Barbara Byers lives and works in Albuquerque with her partner, Margaret Randall. "Because of art," Byers says, "I am alive." She is a master of asemic writing, a maker of artists' books, an explorer of digital painting, and among the most wonderfully out-of-the-blue, productive artists I've ever encountered.

In Guatemala There Are Villages So Small That They Fit within the Crosshairs of a Gun

Benvenuto Chavajay (b. 1978)

Fired clay and painted white wooden platform, 4" x 96", circa 2016

SITElines: New Perspectives on the Art of the Americas (SITE SANTA FE biennial series 2016, entitled "much wider than a line")

On a white slab   laid out   voodoo remains,
what's left   of villages
in crosshairs,   uncountable places missing
in action,   places so small
one gun could do it all;
the evidence now   before us
autopsy toys, pottery   gats, ceramic   six shooters, repeaters
—metaphor,
that's it.

In the crosshairs. Mira.

Gun. Guns. Gunned. Gun down. Gunned down.
      Gunning. Gunning down.

Gunner. Gunman. Gunnery. Gunboat. Gunboat
      diplomacy. Gunrunner.

Arma. Armas. Pistola. Pistolas. Fusil. Balancear.
      Balanceado. Altillo.

Pistolero. Hombre Amado.

Mira! Mira.

Pottery pistols,   effigy play
fakes of killing and maiming,   placebos placed neatly
like teeth, jawbones,   broken femurs poking   out of middens
of catastrophe,   the puzzle remains   of killing fields
plowed up by dozers, backhoes,   leaching up after rain,   remains
displayed for students   with camel-hair brushes
tidying up   grave crumbs on votives of mourning,
milagros of guns jammed, broken,   gunned down
        themselves, a mass
grave of symbolic dead days in precise   patterns of clay
guns, art   guns.   Squint
it's the pattern on a skirt,   look closer it's
viscera and knucklebones, pelvic sockets,   hammer-smashed
toes, nose ridges,   death grins.
Morgue work.

Guns don't pick teeth,
rock babies, tie shoe strings   flapping   undone in mud
        from frantic
bloody running   away, legs tying up
at the very last, nightmare slow,   body in the sights,
mira,   crosshairs,
dead aim,
dead on,
dead sure,   dead.

NOTE: Margaret Randall picked me and a number of other poets to
respond to a work in the SITE 2016 biennial and write a poem for a
wall label. Rini and I went up on July 18, 2016, the week after the
exhibition opened. Many pieces caught my interest. But when I came
upon Chavajay's pottery pistolas, the words just started coming. I
started composing it the night of the 18th and emailed the finished
version back to SITE SANTA FE's Joanne Lefrak, head of education
and outreach.

Seven Deadly Near Misses

When we know we are right, but are not.

(2014)

Taking Credit

It's old as old.
Zeus is quite precise.
Hubris draws the bolt
        of holy indignation. So,
take ownership
of faults and errors, but
the good you do,

        the beauty that seems
to flow from you, the wisdom
that saves your skin, please
know they are
        visitations
and get out of the way.
Hubris slams all doors,

thanks opens the flood.
Does that seem too
self-effacing?
        Oh solipsist. Please do
get out of the way.
All good things, even devotion
to hard work,

come to us from
the great
        Who-Knows-Where.
You don't know,
        surely.
        Do you?
Claiming genius for such gifts

kills them off
comical and fast,
  a trapdoor sprung
under a Persian rug, dropping you
into a pit of midget crocodiles snapping.
Hubris takes credit where credit isn't due,
has the gall to say, "It's me, it's me,

I'm the one. A mystery? Ha!
What a lame excuse." But that's
  claiming you make your own luck.
  It's not the same
as saying she
makes *her* own luck.
That's a form of praise. But to say it

  of yourself
is like saying
you take the credit for your face,
your heart, your voice,
which is, in itself, like saying,
I'm the one who caused
that bright and shiny moon.

Rape

Lust can't help itself, sometimes.
Of course,
      we can
contain ourselves and not
act upon
our bone-white
greed, our fascination,

      and submit
to deep
frustration's moral
swaddling,
      doused
with the ether
the Id exudes

      to subdue itself
tame and dozy as
the Great God Pan
without his terrors.
      But, then,
privilege—ignorance copulating
with arrogance—takes over,

an entitlement to use
libido as a crowbar
to pry
decency apart
      so sex
      and politics and power
seem to belong together,

crossing their wires in the short-
circuiting of conscience,
twisting stupidhappylust into
          a violation of volition
that has no rhyme
or soul, a crime

of impotence
          engorged with status,
as the rapist, like a racist,
forces his image of her
          upon her.
Sex bully mind fucker
he must never not

          win at any cost, smothering
innocence
in ganglia of terror,
Rape
          Is
          No
Escape.

Distraction

Sloth is always saying yes
to nothing.
Distraction is always saying yes
to anything that comes along,
doing, doing, doing,
        doing all at once,
doing as the soul

of doing nothing,
a bustling
vacancy where depth
is fathomless because
        there's nothing
        deep to reach. And so
distracted, we can't

absorb a thing, can't
devote ourselves to anything,
becoming expert
        instead
in deep absences, always
        half drowned
        and gasping in the froth

of The Great Busy Nada.
        Doing frantically,
we becalm ourselves,
sweating to believe
we've done a lot,
a lot! so much,
the list's so long—do this,

do that, do this—so long,
so long, it takes so long
we have
        no time to know, doing
        beyond the forgotten
        and the done,
hoarding action,

stocking up and up,
        nothing on top of nothing,
each nothing so necessary,
        meaningless,
so important, cheap
that a vacuum forms
        the basic

        equation of effort's law:
        all times nothing
equals nothing at all,
doing, doing, doing
a forgery of achievement
        with mocking value
and no end.

Filthy Riches

Gluttony, that slick permissiveness,
morphs into money all the time,
    an inner filthiness
hidden in the linty inside pocket
of the soiled tycoon's tuxedo.
It's building a house with so many rooms
that you can't

    visit half of them in a single day.
    So you must
think of yourself
as an accountant would think
of a great many zeros,
your inner truth
packed like Scrooge's swimming pool

    with doubloons of every kind, enough
for ten lifetimes of stupefying
    just-too-much,
    Rolls-Royces flattened into business cards,
making the valet lug
ten thousand five dollar bills in a bag so you
can buy coffee and scones with a swagger.

To be a scrooge
    is to believe
you are worth your own whims,
that it's right that you have
every last thing that you want,
when you want it,
as you want it

because you think
        you've earned it
        or it proves
Satan's grace, or it just
means you're meaner,
a Darwinian better.
"Give it away?! Are you crazy?!

Deprive some deaf mute
        crippled bastard
on a roller skate cart
of *his* chance to make it all,
        and spend it, too?
Deprive *him*
of his chance at joy, his

swimming pool full of doubloons?
So what if he's got
        not a fat chance
        to jell
his nickels and dimes into billions,
or even a burger and fries.
Don't lay that on *me*!"

Hoarding

Greed can never have enough.
It knows it
        and goes on wanting more.
But hoarding can't
        figure out what enough is.
It's not about filling voids,
about the abhorrence of less, or even

wanting it all, it's about
        riptide impulses
        and foundational stress,
it's a long smothering
        delusion in which
"out of control" is portrayed
as prudence,

as wintering in and stockpiling up.
There it is,
        just what might come in handy,
and you grab it while you can,
even though piles of it are making
just moving around in your house
a dangerous climb in the Alps.

The fear, the surmising of dreads
are always there,
        the relief
        of having enough to buy enough,
a perfection of satisfaction,
a perfect performance, not
        unlike the pen from heaven, or the sentences

no one would change,
which taunt and torment the perfectionist who
would never admit
        to something so foolish and mundane
as the unattainable. But
that euphoric
safety

of the exactly right,
the utterly enough,
can't be dismissed.
        Its longing seeps through every objection,
just the release of having
        exactly what you need
in any crisis, any mad demand of weather

        is a peace that leaves you stuffed
with hollow doubt
        yearning for need. So
store, shelve, pile, accumulate
even though you know you will never run out and might
smother in an avalanche of all
that damnable, sucking stuff.

Celebrity

Envy wants another life.
Celebrity is
the other life it wants.
        Oh smile that warm smile at *me*!
Show those adorable crooked teeth to *me*.
I've touched him. A damp hanky of his
        with his sweat

is in my pocket. Her lipstick on
a cigarette butt is folded
        in a receipt for dog food in my wallet.
I've drunk coffee at the very table where she wrote the tome
that could have changed my life,
but I never read it.
        Celebrities are already

        souvenirs of themselves; they leave us
their leavings.
They step off the screen,
out of the magazine, bump
into us in the grocery store,
appearing in the flesh
in starched French cuffs.

        The myth is at our door:
Achilles asking for a drink of water,
Hector looking for a Band-Aid, Helen wanting
        to borrow your comb for a sec. Only you
have whiffed her breath, have
touched the iced-smooth, voluptuous calm
of her hand with your cheek.

Is it
that everyone wants so much
to be somebody else
that we will
embellish ourselves in the finery
of even someone who has been
        just in the shadow of the great?

Is that the allure?
        The celebrated trying
to be as normal as
those who touch them so
they won't have to be
utterly normal anymore?
Would it be the same

if one day you saw
Hitler buying shoes, Pinochet
checking his fly, or Stalin
        squeezing melons?
Not quite, would it?
A sharp, fast
        knife would do.

Judgment

Anger eliminates
the rest of us. It literally
        replaces us.
Judgment,
        accusing
        or tisk-tisking others, is not
a raging but

an ermine
savagery,
        a cloying fraud, a casting
of the first stone, |
tormenting others
        who we know
the Holy tells us

are ourselves
        in different faces.
And our own selves inside?
Hypocrites without mercy,
        jeering at those fools
        in the baited traps
        of our mirrors,

as the righteous quicksand of our blame
        pulls us flailing under.
And even then
we see no similarity
though we have been told
        again and again
we are the same.

And we destroy this likeness
          in the name of accusation
so we purge our own
likeness of ourselves
of any sympathy, refusing to be
self-accused.

          Going to a hanging
and feeling safe, escaping detection,
mesmerized to watch
          the terrible bastard climb the steps,
          we look away when he turns
and smiles our smile, trembling
in the truth of our own

          terrible near-crimes
          by any other name.
In the middle of the night
our hearts pound like the man
who feels the noose
before he feels
the drop.

NOTE: The Seven Deadly Near Misses are a sequel to the Seven Deadly Sins. They are not exactly further refinements, nor are they lesser variants. They are parts of the spectrum of fallibility that each of the Seven Deadlies occupies.

The Others

HE COULD SEE
the long pattern now;
writing and learning
would be the measure
of his peace of mind.
The tasks would add up.
The details would crowd,
the pressures of "production"
would expand—
and that's as he would have it
for as long as he could have it.
Writing well, thinking clearly,
never missing a chance to expand and grow
all abstractions, to be sure—but all are there
to be filled with the right
content. Content was
and is all.

ILLNESS IS NOT
an instrument of politics,
a tool, a device to get what you need
and what life won't give you otherwise.
Illness isn't useful
unless your life is so sick
it needs it.
Be careful. Illness is real.
The sources, causes are real.
The physical miseries are real—but
there are two factions, if you will:
the real uncaused by you
and the fictitious (real symptoms, real tumors, real pain)
that serves other purposes,

choice by other means.
When you can't choose,
you can create situations
in which you have no choice.

EVERYTHING DEPENDS
on the right way of thinking.
You do not have to hurt yourself
to get what you want and need.
You do not have to create
circumstances in which
you have no choice
but to do what you couldn't choose
but wanted to.
Freedom is not
a nullity, not a nihilism,
not to be derived
from a negative.
You may get what you want,
but the price is vast
and destroys the benefit.

IN A UNIVERSE
in which the way to entropy
takes infinite, horrified form
in which you can feel
in yourself "disorganization"
going on,
the only actual
factual
refuge

that exists
is now
as it evolves
now as it is,
now as it just was,
now the imperishable,
now like Athena
impervious to Aphrodite,
now impervious
to entropy
that uses it as its stream
of distinction.

HOLDING HER HAND
hearing her mutterings
and gentle howlings
knowing she's trying
to wrap up her life
and leave it behind
or is it just making the sounds
of dying, we'll never know.
We see our own ends,
in hall mirrors, still dark and far away
to our sight—we know what will happen
is there, but we don't know
how or when, even though
we can see its form, however barely,
however dimly, and hear this image say
now is your refuge, worry not,
be ceaselessly grateful.
Live. I am coming.

THE ANCHORING GOOD SPIRIT
has departed—the magnetic cheer
and toleration—the person
with so many problems of her own
who kept them to herself
and kept happiness going
where it mattered—even while
her demons sliced at her
and walled her in behind
her stashes of impregnable stuff:
the paradox of the moon
and its invisible dark side:
with her, both made the whole
what it was and had to be—
nourishment and worried joy.

VIRGIL WHO
as a Roman, lived
with death daily,
lived, caused, mourned,
ignored death daily.
Virgil knew the truth about it
right down to the nerves
of his lyre. Death plucks
my ear, he says.
Waste not a breath, stress
not over guesses.
Waste not a moment now
worrying about then.

HE COULD SEE
himself accumulate
small ills, some of them
causing great pain,
all of them needed
to be managed,
but the press of his life,
his work and art
and family and society
of deep friends
pushed him along so the ills
were more like sucker fish
than the shark chewing
into his rib cage.
There is no formula.
Just live your joy.
Let it take the lead.
But don't be
a fool with pain.

HE UNDERSTOOD
that to be who he is
he had to change,
but he had never put
all the advice together.
Change. Relax. Be still.
Now is your refuge.
Worry not.
Never cease being grateful.

Don't identify.
Self-actualize.
That's what it takes,
he thought, to be
who I am,
naturally, easygoing,
naturally calm and
naturally grateful.
Unworried.

HE WAS SO
resistant to change,
it repelled him so
convincingly that
to see it as a condition
of authentic being,
of being who he is,
almost slipped
right by him.
But there it was,
the admonition, advice,
the answer that could
not be denied, and must
not be overlooked.
Change must be
made your own. You know
what's easy to change?
Patterns of consumptions.
You know that
when you change them,
other changes will harden and resist.

HE THOUGHT HIS WAY
out of the traps.
He was humble enough
to accept help,
stupid enough to follow it
only infrequently,
wise enough to keep on trying.
He knew he had a long way to go,
that if he got sick
he would have to navigate
between the standard
and the revolt
and would do so
by asking for help
and learning to follow
the answers when
all they require
is practice once
you think they are
right and true
enough to stake
your life on.

HE KNEW WHAT
was right—somewhat—
or at least whose side
he was on.
That was clear to him.
But he didn't know
it he would feel regret
for killing the ogre

attacking him and his friends
if he'd feel remorse
if he'd even comprehend
that the ogre was more
than he seemed—perhaps
gentle at heart
but made huge and deadly
by hate. So
when you kill the ogre
attacking you, he wants
to kill all of you, and
you kill all of him first.
Ogre, ogre, wherefore
art thou ogre?

HE KNEW HIS BEST
ideas came to him
by chance and whim,
by sideways glancing,
like fame comes
when you turn away
and shun the effort.
He picked up Keats
on a whim, read of
nightingales and urns
and psyche and love
we know without the
slightest mercy,
and came to imagination
again as a source
of truth, unaccountably,
to the liberating and

pedestrian insight on how
to organize his days
like laying bricks.

HE KNEW NOW
what he had to do—
he knew he had to do
all the moves
he'd never brought
himself to make
before—he'd have
to do what had come
to seem impossible
to do. He'd have to do
what he could not do
and had not done before.
He'd have to break
a barrier, leap a gorge
but he'd have to find
a way to try without
guaranteeing the usual
failure. He would
have to vault
without leaping.

HE COULD SEE NOW
that he had to spend
so much energy just
to maintain order
and direction that
he couldn't afford.

Literally his energy
wallet was so
empty after essential
efforts that he couldn't
afford his useless
troubles anymore
his prideful loathing
of his own incapacities.
He had to give up
wanting to be
who he was not
and who he had always
refused to be despite
the tisk-tisking
of false guilt
in his false conscience.
What he could do
had at least become
more important than
what he couldn't.

IF NOW IS MY REFUGE
he thought, how can I be
concerned with the future
or the past? Both are
absolutely beyond
my influence or desire.
Certainly, yes, you can
prepare now for what
you think will probably,
given the odds, happen
as you age in nows to come.

But do your plans,
any more than your desires
for recognition, have
anything to do
with the future? Only
insofar as the future
you will have depends
on you. Plans, if you do them,
often pan out, desires
for recognition and
acceptance depend
on others and they
are beyond your influence
even now and always
then. It's hard to charm them
from the grave with what
you haven't done.

HE KNEW MOMENTUM
always flagged,
that it needed a shot
almost every day, some
renewed boost, but
where could he find it,
where could it come from?
Did he have to make it
himself? Did new energy
come from dreaming it up,
like he dreamed himself
up so long ago—was imagination
and desire the source
the actual source of new

momentum, renewed
energy? Was this
alchemy real? His whole
life said yes,
yes,
yes.

FROM EACH ACCORDING TO HIS ABILITY
to each according to his need,
even there I am not a materialist.
When the physicist says
the beauty of science is its lack
of subjectivity, materialism rears
its razor-thin head about what
matter makes that is beyond matter
—love, ideas, metaphysics, music, poetry,
Rini's magnificent dance with the unknown
appearing from the tip of her pencil.
Is matter primary and "subjectivity" next?
Politics without subjectivity
is the brutality of tyranny: the tyrant
and his ideas are
the only subjects that matter.

CERTAIN "FRIENDS"
put dampers on you.
Oh, I suppose, all "friends"
put dampers on you,
all situations, all contexts.

Being who you are without
being boorish is
a delicate matter, if you consider
other people are
as important as you.
Be who you are. Change!
Stop hiding behind anonymity.
You are a poet, a reader
of Elizabeth Sewell and the classics,
an autodidact, polymath ignoramus,
a person of opinions. Perhaps
I should remain loyal and forget
all about the dismissers and the one-uppers.

TO BE WHO YOU ARE
means, he thought, to follow,
to actually do the advice
you asked to receive,
to actually do what the
indwelling voice has said to do.
When you in fact try
to forgive, and really do it,
you change the same as you change
when you find your refuge
in now, and in purpose and order.
You change as much as you do
when you trust and don't mind.
The wisdom of humility is not
confusing obedience with being wise.

HE WAS COMING TO UNDERSTAND
that a log jam might be
breaking up inside him,
that life was swirling and changing
and that the speed was so
powerful it simply had started
to shudder the jam.
He knew that whatever happened now
he could not pretend to be
who he was not. He had to learn
and be who he was, who he is
without animosity
but with generous candor.

THE RENDING OF THE FABRIC
of a way of life that is now former
creates, he thought, a vortex of grief
into which rushes all the unfinished
business of dealing with death
over and over again—and coming
to the realization of having to deal
with the disappointment of your own
death, in its way, cloaked in its mystery.
He allowed himself to fall into
the rabbit hole and feel everything
that was there to be felt. He didn't
land in Wonderland, but the result
caused him to wonder about the fall
and about innocence regained.

YOU THINK YOU CAN'T
possibly do it, that it can't
possibly be done
in the time you have
even though you've done it
thousands of times, literally
thousands and thousands of times,
he thought to himself. The secret
is to use whatever and all
the time you have, even if it is
spare time—a whole body of work,
a whole creative "career"
can be built from spare time.
Spare time is enough to build a lifetime
of work, of satisfaction, of fulfillment,
even if it never felt good doing it,
never seemed enough,
was worryingly haggard,
haggard time, a lifetime
better than no time.

THE TALKING CURE WORKS
because the mind believes
what it says, just as it believes
its images and its
metaphors, just as it is healed
by new connections, new insight
new relationships uncovered
between this idea and that.

That is why negativity is
so dangerous, so beyond
help, because the mind
believes itself, it even believes
its tricks, and tends to believe
and feel and do what it is
told. The rule must be, he thought,
say what you want and who
you are in your own
best interest and you could
become what you say, as sure
as the mind has weather
the climate of thought
determines it.

WE ARE PRESIDING AGAIN
over the end-of-the-way-it-has-been,
and taking the first steps into a world-as-it-is-now,
a world as yet still very like the old one,
but with lava and ice and wind and flood
chewing, digesting the far
edges of our calm, like cosmic monsters
eating a galaxy from the outside inward,
or a sea of acid vanishing a living island
from its coastline in—this is where we are
and this is how we shall always be until
time chews us away, leaves in grasshoppers' jaws.

NOTHING MATTERS,
he thought, but the care of others
and the care of yourself
for others.
He found that strange to say.
But it did appear beneath his pen point;
the narcissistic mind,
where you are all
that matters, leaves you
without a reason, without
a purpose, without a meaning
as an isolate, a spark in the void.
When you care for yourself
for others, and care for others
for yourself, you belong
to the human island, you are
of the species, a spark
itself in the void, but a spark
that is in
with billions and billions.

YOU JUST HAVE TO TRUST
in the goodness
of people you admire,
he thought,
not in their competence,
their wisdom, just

their goodness
and you have to trust
the future will unfold
as it will, not as you try
to predict it and certainly
not as you would like it to be.
It's all a matter of simpatico
with the universe,
with friends, with who
you know people to be
and what you know
of their strengths. Just
trust.

HE KNEW TO NEVER
take credit
for anything.
The good
that happened to him,
and that came from him,
was not because
he was good or deserving,
he could not think that,
good is everywhere
and he just happened
into it, and got out of its way
from time to time—
by hard work, yes
of course, but the work
wasn't all that hard
and he didn't have
a definable goal except

to get better, repair
ignorance, and try to be
a good person
for no other reason than
he wanted to be
on the side of love
and kindness
and generosity,
for no other reason
than he didn't want
the alternative.

EVERYTHING IS PASSING
on, passing away,
in constant flux, precious
one second
junk and carcass the next.
We know this, of course.
Even Freud fleeing
the Gestapo knew
that to them he was
nothing but a bag of bone
and slippery guck
walking around,
getting in the way,
ready for the garbage pail
of Auschwitz. And the most
fragile things of all,
our interiority, the secret
worlds we all inhabit, the very
ground for the sacredness
of the holy soul, the wholly

irreplaceable, one-of-a-kind
human self sacred as anything
else in the Cosmos is—
vulnerable as mice in the field,
as leaves whirling in the breeze,
as ants trouping on the sidewalk,
and all this we cherish
—the stage of our lives,
our rocks, our pens, our shirts,
our photographs and gardens,
our books and notes
all upon our last breath,
just trash for some relative
to worry over and finally
to sweep away out the door,
weeping perhaps
but relieved.

WE ARE OR WE ARE NOT
in the foyer of
the apocalypse,
enjoying our
espresso, our
caprese, our
meatballs
in balsamic
reduction,

our fake
cigarettes
to calm
us down,
our mysterious
pens and
soft old shirts.
The door from the foyer
has not opened all the way
for sixty-nine years. It's
cracked, it's hung ajar
far too often to say
it is normally closed.
The nurse
euthanizing
the old, the hale,
the maimed,
the scatter-headed
has not popped
out to issue forth
her coo-coo call
to action, but we
patients in our billions
know she's preparing
the needles, the hoses,
the clamps, the jugular
vices as we speak.

THE MIRROR OF LOVE
has a funhouse warp.
It mirrors every flaw,
the eccentric boy-man becomes
a monster of rude
disregard, a freak
of dismissal, banishing
all from the razor
cruel absolutes of his
needs and attention.
But know he is,
in another mirror
of love, an interpersonal
cripple, socially demented,
unable to express real love
because he does not
feel it, only know what it
should be like—in the final
mirror of love, with no warp,
no distortion, he is a fine
person, a man of conscience
and a sense of justice,
a man of high humor who one wants
to be loved by because
we love him, but who instead
meows and lurks and keeps
his fearful distance until we leave
and he gets what he needs
with no one in the way.
But whereas eccentric cats
are charming, eccentric apes

are grasping, self-righteous
and often boorish, who throw
their shit at you from the trees.
Certainly, wear a hat
and protective gear, investigate
them and then
don't let them get
anywhere near you.

UP FROM THE DEPTHS
comes the demon of hate,
the Eichmann in man,
the monster of disproportion,
turning irritation, or arrogance,
or mild revulsion into murderous
overkill. The demon
is a Moloch with a mouth of fire
and eyes like buzz saws
seeing nothing but the gore
of its own satisfaction,
the girl with the blue plastic bags,
the SS sadist, Stalin's torturers,
the inquisitive devils of Christ,
the throat-slitters of Islam,
the witch-hangers of Salem,
in their own minds, first-stone
throwers to a person as clean of sin
as a viper or a shark is clean
of their genes that make them kill,
in their own minds, in their own minds.

AGNUS MARTIN
turned her back
to the world
and became famous
in the world for making
graph paper paintings
that the world did not
comprehend until
she told them
they were about the peace
of turning your back
to the world
that makes you famous.
(Are two sides of the same coin
always as idiotic and obvious?
Physics and chemistry
are on the same coin,
but love and hate
are two coins
with nothing
else on either side.)

WHEN YOU DO UNTO OTHERS
what you would have them do
unto you, he thought, you cut
them slack, always, for everything,
you forgive, you forget unless
they try to harm you, then you
ward them off without
condemnation, neutralize them
somehow, keep them away,
and if you can't, then you must

exert anger, as an impulse,
not a righteous myth—spare them
your fantasies of evil if you must
do them in, quick as you would
like them to do unto you.

LIFE HAD MADE HIM SO JUMPY
he knew that even the cat,
even the eccentric washing machine pinging,
could made his blood pressure
pounce into the doctors' danger zone,
even just looking at the limbs
of trees swaying in a good breeze
could make him fret paralytically
about his roof. He knew he was
so jumpy because life had
nicked him in the ear, the back, the knee,
the tender spots of love
that bleed so easily, that he was just
ready and waiting for the worst
in every passing tick and crunch and meow.

DEPRESSION, HE WONDERED,
is it just "wrong thinking" or is it
just "chemistry" and an "internal
imbalance"? Is it just
weakness and giving in
to an internal midnight, or is it
a true response to the way
the world really is?
A piling-up of tiny insights

into the carnage and horror,
and sadism and chaos of living
as a life, a conscious life, in a world
of voracious unconscious forces
that in themselves feel no pain
while inflicting pain
as their major byproduct
after gaining-eating-devouring-consuming
what they want.
Depression in the face of people
tortured to death for their thoughts
is not a weakness, not a mere
diagnosis.

EGO
like a Chinese box
each of us
nested in a
bigger one
that we attempt to
outgrow, overwhelm, supersede.
But ego and fame
are not the same thing
and do not feed off
the same powers.
Fame is the illusion of others.
Ego has a goal, however
juvenile, to feed the illusions
of others with what is important
to it, not what is important to them.

(2014)

Specimen Poems

18 April 2014

desert willow entrances
light from the river bank
poetry woven through the wind in grass stalks
where is the cat and the robins
how fair are the jays and Cooper's hawks
the Maximilians flood the dirt with green in its emphatic calm

19 April 2014

sinners lapidary
smooth, porphyry marble
slabs surrounding the hall
dark crystal caves—the errors made
turn gem to stone if no harm is known
or done to others but
yourself, an ordeal, a test,
a metamorphic stone being fused by time and insight.
be good to the world.
God forgive us, as we forgive others.
of harmony.
that is the Law

20 April 2014

a Veronal doze
in bonnie Brazil on a cot
asleep for the ages
the great man snoring dead
the great man's amanuenses
dead cold head on his chest
Nazis cheering at these

premature departures
breaking the deep stalactites in the geode
with a screwdriver wiggled in a hole
just for the sake of doing it, any it you please
scratching the silver box top
with a nail file
in a child's fantastic rage

21 April 2014

water so pure
you could be born into it,
oil, gas, solvents, nukes
like snow in a snow globe
falling through the liquid birth pool overhead
a placental sky ozone burned away;
leave clean or clean up
that is not a question.
universal solvents liquefy
vast assets into being
and who cares what comes next?

22 April 2014

blast, smoke, blood
death on the asphalt
chased, fired, killed
matrix of defiance
indifference
I'll show you like rutile
darting motionless through crystal
the girl nineteen

her head smashed to the ground,
her skull bounded
someone will cut her apart
saw open her skull
remover her viscera
find bullets perhaps
her father crumpled
like a wadded paper bag on the floor

23 April 2014

the big vault door
is shut tight, tons
of steel between us
and the answer
questions have no leverage against it
no whiff of dissent can seep
through the edges.
are they locked in
or are we locked out?
will we ever know?
our titanium teeth
and hip joints
will of course last longer
than our bones.
time and truth
slammed shut.
the grass over here
senses the hole in the sky
but the big door won't budge
and when you set around it
there's nothing but a smooth
air landscape there

24 April 2014

rock hard black crystal
mass lead heavy
with a dark rest fleshy
secret disease in its
weightiness
ocean curling
star dazzle
darkness and the flesh
pit inside expanding
killing stone, stomping out
the blank, the nerveless
rock, feeling it quiver
even evil has its death sobs
obsidian edges dull up fast on bone

25 April 2014

tornado tunnel
tearing ground, grinding
houses, cars, baby
buggies into mulch. Inside
the tunnel calm
as the edge of a knife
is sharp, lethal,
without agitation,
just what it is
no more, no worries, keen
so clean, it is
sharpness itself,
smooth and thinner
than big muscle, paper, skin
can bear

26 April 2014

found at the end of a world
where no one is but
us and them,
an oasis of weather
and a way of thought,
thinking as a landscape
that make us go its way,
like gravity makes rivers,
like rolling hills hide creeks,
and we go as the thought land flows

27 April 2014

expectations shooting
through the geode
crystals of distortion
rocks are what they are
without intrusions
of other form
cavernous selves dripping time
huge piles of it,
shocking inner caverns
when light is shone
the intrusions are either
yours by adaptation or
they are girders, stents,
crammed, jammed, forced
into the space of you
—nature changes
as it must, expectation
forces and distorts

28 April 2014

nurturing talent,
not chipping away detritus
to reveal true form
others do that
polishing is your job
self-polished, eroded
by history, sea stone
smoothed with tides,
never identify, never
help others to
identify, just to
polish, to make
actual their form

29 April 2014

gun metal mouth
spewing dust, the hole
of the hiders, tunneling
down, tunneling away
from the light, the sun,
the press, smoking gun
mouth silent, sewed shut
a shrunken head leading
the parade of the mangled
where is the puppeteer?

30 April 2014

boiling neurons spiced
with heather and salt cedar
in the breezes, roiling
fears beneath the calm,
amid the toy soldiers
with real guns and tiny
piercing bullets—fear
of sickness, fear of police,
fear of the knock at the door,
fear that put Benjamin
to sleep forever—unbearable
being born, escaping into
expensive and dangerous
habits, in the end
it was the bacon, as one poet said

1 May 2014

the core of culture
a knot in a log
thou shalt not kill
the law most often
broken, a wine glass
blown by angelic youth
to such exquisite
thinness they ring
of death, like the bell
on the dog leading us home
up the avenue
of the agonies

2 May 2014

thou shalt not kill
road signs covered
in asphalt and gravel
twisted by coal truck
monsters and police
department tanks,
little flutters of twinkie
cellophane smeared
black, some pigeon down,
an old raven squawking
off traffic, picking at
what seems to be
human toes

3 May 2014

ego wells
polluted by fame
and rejection—
the concave and
convex they bollox
any sex, they go
like slack knuckles
on trains one on the other,
ego the precious

semi wondrous, almost
gemstone treasured
only by you in your
pinpoint infinite solipsism
how many standing ovations
on the head of a pin
how many rejection slips
stuffing the scarecrow

4 May 2014

fear smearing
your leg, the
stink of it,
a molten freeze
flowing fast,
not glacial
but frozen lava
grooming secrets,
flooding the garden
escaping into
the street where
waste will be
noticed and shame
will glisten
like snot
running into
your moustache

5 May 2014

slag piles, leaden
clouds, mercury
jet streams
slick in the weather,
the climate so hard,
so fluid, so relentlessly
an avalanche of anvils
swooping through
the willow meadows
and always, just above,
stratigraphy of vapors
so heavy, so
flagstone dense
none of the grasses
turn green
yellowed, a broken
home for the roaches
and the roly polies

6 May 2014

luck granite
veins, sparklers
from the molten
core, heavy beyond
heat, absolute as
the speed of light,
mercurial, hermetic
chance machines
invisible clunking

through the history
of coincidence, chugging
away behind the sky—
not even holy repair
men know
what will happen
when the chance
machine starts up again

7 May 2014

apple wet
inside out
sweet wet
no rot,
no worm,
aged to
just right,
catch it
now, catch
your life
now.
the great marble
cube, perfect
for the head
and face of
god. one false
blow and it
cracks uselessly.
one dumb

mistake is all
it takes.
but risk
it all, that's
all it takes.
the mistake is
not to risk
mistakes

8 May 2014

Days are clamping down,
boxes full of life
corded, strapped shut,
sealed-new boxes
far fewer, the assembly
line endless long ago is now
coming to an edge
not an end but a
new level. The boxes are
dropping down
and moving on, full
of good things, but the gold
still processed above is
stacking up and needs
to fill the not-so-endless
rest of time.

9 May 2014

trapped in a matrix
seemingly at one
with it, radiant,
amazed, more profound
than sunlight distilled
into the dawns of all the planets
moving around all the stars,
still trapped in matrix,
in galactic glories that are not
what you think you are,
nor think you must do;
matrix rules without revolt
then revolt shatters all
just to be free, free
with nothing left

10 May 2014

What is missing is
in its not-there-ness.
Absence has
a being, if not
a presence, though it is
present in its being gone.
Great avalanche
over the road.
The road is there
but is no longer a road.
It will be
and it was, but its

absence now, its state
of being missing
makes room for
the avalanche
which caused its
absence a way to get
from here to there.
Just do not be
one of the missing
always there
but never coming back.

11 May 2014

miles stored up
in engines and
the power of the will
to follow them.
who knew one brain
would unfold
untold thousands
upon thousands
of ideas and poems
and essays. who knew
the potential of the stone
in David's sling?

12 May 2014 – Cortez, Colorado

Time travel
asphalt engine
wind, great sleek
sleepy speed, from
one place to
another, one time
from another, you can
only tell you have
arrived when you get there
often just as you are leaving.
Strip mall desert
wind storm, ozone smog,
pyres of stone channeling
fire of time
in our bodies
as we move across
the planet's turning,
spinning of the
numbers, spilling
of the dust.

13 May 2014 – Price, Utah

The road unravels,
the knotted and the tangled,
the rubber band self-strangled
around a long, single ratted
strand of family. A hair in the
back of your throat. But
old hurts fall away
like fruit from seed
too sweet but new
and real enough to be
believed, unrequited feelings,
old anger at old sleights,
rotten, spoiled,
restraining with repugnance,
not all gone,
but spilling out
like a red carpet
rolling for miles and centuries.

14 May 2014 – Kemmerer, Wyoming

throat sore
great cloggy avalanche
of mucus glacial
movement of the tensions
of the year struggling
to exit the head,
exit the cells, dead

sister, dead friends, work
house stress, getting
old, not knowing it
a big tree so sturdy, so
time tested over and over at
boot camps of beginnings
and changings; are the limbs
hollowing out, are the leaves
this year just one leaf
too much, will he snap
only the fall
or not
will tell

15 May 2014 – Idaho Falls, Idaho

geodes, the geode of a life,
the hard miseries, tornados
of the surface; we identify
with the rock and grime,
the corpses of fortune
on the surface and then
we see we are more
apparently we can feel it
inside, feel ourselves
at the core; the surface must
not be cracked, never violence,
we see by feeling not by touch,
it is us but never by force, never
by instruction

16 May 2014 – Missoula, Montana

a dark choice,
an accident that causes
reality to change, a role
that must be hidden
but played to the full—a spy,
a plant, a snitch in the midst
of liars and thieves
all tanged in truth and the horrible
might-have-beens and still-might-bes,
mysteries unraveling
into knots of new
quandaries, "fresh hells"
and puzzles—that is the terrible
cement of chance that hardens
when your answers becomes questions
that challenge
the answers that caused them

17 May 2014 – Essex, Montana

wearing brick
glasses with tiny cracks;
can't see much
and your eyes feel
dusty with grit
skipping stones are
long gone
in their rings, no sight
through them—attitudes
sand blast vision,

determine mood
nothing is real
behind the brick walls
now we know the wall
we're trapped behind
can be just
kicked out; it's only brick
an illusion of substance
free as scree
sloping down
the perfect hill of perfect pines
is always there
to be seen
if you can

18 May 2014 – Choteau, Montana

windshield dust
so thick for a while
the driver was a sleep walker
guided by the fairy of good luck,
the car a sanatorium
moving through the days moving
through the places
the windshield big bay window
was cleaned by
inclement days so
it sparkled and the driver
woke up just in time
to slip by the eighteen-wheeler
whose driver was drifting off
and drifting over into his lane

19 May 2014 – Ennis, Montana

questions morphing
into answers—what's true,
what's not, empirical evidence,
calculations,
twistings, denyings—creating
categories of answers
designed like a magic trick
to convince with confusion.
How do you know?
How can you be sure?
You see something happen,
someone says something will happen
or has happened, and it's like
the bent fork trick—the tines are
bent—but how or when
is not clear—the causes are not clear—
a big stone cut and polished
into millions, but just a big stone
or a particular kind of stone.
Which is the truth?
Both and more.

20 May 2014 – Pinedale, Wyoming

An edifice is built
around deficiencies
forgiven.
There is not rot, shame,
and harm in the future
if forgiveness does not win.

But forgiving one's past,
one's self is a prelude to
having no righteous
judgment about
anyone else alive.
The geode opens to find
flaw upon miraculous flaw
building into a miracle
of substance. Only
forgiveness makes this
real.

21 May 2014 – Lander, Wyoming

Scrambled head
unconscious streams and
sulfur geysers, fissures
oozing thought
pus all released
by fiction—by the
hammer of a new project,
striking the mind
geode open to get at
plot and character
and opening more than
what is needed, releasing
extra savorings, the kitchen
of imagination working
without receipt, and we must
take the good with
the very bad and not
get mental salmonella.
Don't go there!
Do go here.

22 May 2014 – Laramie, Wyoming

A galaxy
in a BB
rattling around
in a marble
in a pocket
of a child
living on a
planet so
infinitesimal
and so
monumental
that it vanishes
in a diamond
full of galaxies
on the finger
of a god who
thinks she is
eternal, ruling
a puff of dust
with universes
swirling. Of course
we don't and can't
know enough,
of course
our stories are
absurd. Trust,
trust, trust.
Even the Dao
is a splinter
of time.

23 May 2014 – Saratoga, Wyoming

The stress gets into
your cells, sleepless
stress, sleepless
protein matter,
sleepless stone,
dead at rest.
The great gray
electronic universe
in our skulls
compensates, tries
to teach the body
that it's all alright.
Mind knows
it's okay, okay now
as always. Mind knows
the stars don't care
but something inside
its grayness and
beyond it does.
It advises:
Relax.
Can stress
relax?

24 May 2014 – Leadville, Colorado

Chance works
spinning and catching,
snaring and missing,
the car off the road
a crumpled smear,
clothes and luggage
flopped over
the embankment.
Opening the Gideon
randomly to
Ecclesiastes 9:12.
Accident? Guidance?
More, vastly more,
so much more
than we can know,
pretend to know
under the sun.
When the wheels
within wheels
within gears within
pulleys, galaxies-wide
and -deep,
move in your direction,
the enigma machine
of chance spells out
your name, then spells
a million others
with their own
times and dates and hows,

almost like yours,
all you can do is
trust what you
have been given
to know, that it is
good.

25 May 2014 – Salida, Colorado

Done, over,
ended with a startling
shadowing
finality.
The huge stone
jagged,
cracked
on the road, its
mountain life
ended, the start
now of a billion
years of change,
and a billion
more, eroding
into a smooth
stone for a pocket,
an amulet
of the cosmos
as it changes
endlessly to be
what it is.

26 May 2014 – Albuquerque, New Mexico

Warp speed crystals inner
rivers gorged with time
and work overflowing
banks and the peace of order
with shaking hands
much too much
to handle, much too much
to do. Trying to find
the peace of mind
the uncluttered simple
flat rock, the big, warm
slab to lie on and
calmly say
what is in me to be said.

(2014)

Material Follies

*For young writers and artists
trying to keep afloat.*

(2015)

Squandering

It's the fulfillment of whims,
the robotic gushing of money, of time

spurting out, cascading, vanishing for nothing
as if you will always have enough

of everything—you're just a programmed
culprit of what you abhor,

a modified spigot that won't turn off,
trained by madmen to want

what you've never thought of
even once before, enticed by design, by the chic

war for your psyche, prying you apart
with machines of art you can't resist

like hiking your arm at a Nuremberg rally
and all to be like the mere actors

who sell you the goods, praising detergents,
magic sweepers as if they were sightings

of the Virgin sparkling in the dungeon
of sponges and cleaners under the sink.

The opposite, wasting not, adds time to things
and makes them smoother, softer,

more and more reliable. Of course
things break down, succumb

to their weakest parts.
But that takes a lot of meantimes.

When they're gone, though,
that's all there is, there isn't any more.

Use what you can
till you can't. Time likes that.

Tempting Fate

Living a free-fall, high-wire life,
rock-face climbing without a rope,

one failure the only failure, living like that,
without any help from yourself, is suicide

by optimism. Great work is a lifetime thing.
It's not a Russian roulette of success

with only one chamber empty.
Daredevil living dooms to the void

the work that would keep unfolding
as long as you're there

to receive it. This requires no
James Bond technology, no machine guns

from tailpipes, catapult seats.
Piggy banks would do just fine.

Do what the work demands, of course.
But don't let it kill you. This is not

superspy smart, just kid stuff really,
but what agony comes

from being without, running on empty
when you know you have

so much left to be said
and made and understood.

When you've saved a lot, it seems
you rarely need a drop of it.

When you've not, fate takes advantage. But don't
save love, or good ideas, or perfect images.

Use them all up.
There's no rainy day for them.

Hoarding

So well prepared
for the eventualities

of her imagination,
she couldn't move

out of the way of the real
boulder

crashing down
through the trees.

She tried to run, to step aside
but the pounds of toilet paper, canned tuna,

eyebrow pencils, lipsticks, nitroglycerine pills,
videos shored up against disaster

and dips into destitution
tripped her up with every step.

She had so much stuff
she couldn't budge, homeless

even in her storehouse car.
There was just no way

to see past her preparations
as she drove along the mountainside,

the windshield obscured
except for a tiny hole,

and no side vision.
Pathologically prepared,

obliteration
by the eighteen-wheeler

actually took no
preparation at all.

Micromanaging

Ordering creates
inspiring space

so what would happen
can happen. Turning molehills

into sweat shops, though,
simulates flow.

Mock-ups are all you get.
Control without grace,

it squeezes particulars
into cramped

spaces of intention. It is
the opposite of trust,

of making humble room
for the ever unforeseen. It jams up

flow with effort—it substitutes
intention for direction,

even for indirection
with a purpose. It limits chances

and crams the urge
of the universe into the limits

of neurosis and history
instead of giving us ways

to ride the unknown into fluorescence
after fluorescence. Trust is the greatest

discipline. See what is, go with it, and
when it's wrong, trust

there's another way
and that you can find it.

Force

Force is not just
for politics by other means.

When you force yourself to be
who you want to be, and you can't

get there, it's not unlike being open
to the fatal blow to the ear,

the dagger in the crotch,
the final defeat from false

information. Force must not fail.
When it does, the artful

detonate from frustration.
Try to force art like a paper Narcissus,

try to force what can only
come from the madness of the gods,

and you've stood on the toes
of glorious muses. Paperweights

will be your only reward.
Force may win out, but if it does

expect only the very, very
worst to be the achievement.

There's a secret: clear the desk,
be in the safe garret of your dreams,

smell apple peels in the drawer,
have three inks and four perfect pens

if that's what it takes, if that's what opens
and clears the way and allows who you are

to change and relax into your being without
the slightest nudge from your needy intentions.

All Your Eggs in One Basket

The way of the world will never
suffer the burden of your needs.

It will do what it does,
its fat-headed this-and-thats,

and leave you flatfooted to meet
what always comes at you

out of the blue. Do not presume.
Toss the ball bat hard, twirling up

and churning in air. It will smack you
dead on, on the back of your head, dead

just because you presumed you could catch it.
Go ahead—humble yourself,

prepare for the wrecking ball
smashing into your office, the concrete slab

falling onto your car from a freeway bridge,
the market rotted and collapsing.

But even with many baskets stashed in many places,
they could all go up in smoke if they are

too close together, almost one, not clearly many.
Multiplicity, variety, plurality. Diversify

your escape routes, your fakeries that lead
to credibility. Trust only that chance

will tap your shoulder once
before it leaves, or ram your head

into the nail sticking out
behind the cat food in the garage

when you fall from the bottom step
because you didn't hold onto the rail.

The Seven Tempting Virtues
(2015)

Chastity

The clean of heart are not absent of any taint,
nor free of rage, nor loosed from wanton teetering
into what temptation really is—doing what you know

you would not want to do when you know
who you really are. The chaste, the wholly honest
without malice, are free not of error, nor of missing the mark,

but free of the desire to harm, to proclaim their purity,
to shame, to hold it up to others. When taint becomes
their terror, though, they see impurity even where it's not,

see innocence and its merriments as sinister beyond
redemption, which they condemn with an ignorant
thrilling zeal as they puff and flex in their hypocrisy, casting

stone upon stone upon stone, amen, cosmically
deranged, deluded, self-important, self-condemned.

Charity

It's The Rule, of course, so pure, so absolutely simple.
Give what they need to those who need it. Don't ask why.
Give money, presence, your true attention. Show up

even if it isn't what you want. This is not a selflessness.
We must give to ourselves what we need,
not just what we crave. And we need to give,

although charity can be bewitched into a way
to give ourselves nobility, some elevation in our eyes,
cork lifts in our shoes, forcing our gift as we want to give it

on those who may not want it that way at all.
Peevish do-gooding grandiosity pollutes intent,
that's why Big Deal giving is not charity.

It's philanthropy. Such a big word. Caritas is small,
immediate, invisible, and forgotten.

Temperance

It's one thing to force yourself—that's hard enough—
to be self-disciplined, productive when you must
or can't help yourself, vitalized by the muse's lust.

But the opposite—refraining, tempering, restraining,
avoiding, abstaining—how do you get yourself to stop
doing what you do not want? And why don't you want it?

Is it clutter, waste, being "bad" for yourself and for others?
Or is it that temperance is the gateway to superiority?
The expectation that others will follow, throwing the first

abstention at a wanton wretch, nagging the addicted
because they look weak and loose, judging as if
virtue really was the reward for good intentions.

When temperance is achieved it's because the tempting
has ceased to be temptation. No big deal.

Diligence

It's true. All that matters is the effort,
the trying that morphs into works.
There's talent, of course, and serving others,

but without doing, day in and month out,
motive and intent add up to nothing.
Diligence is the fuel that feeds the law

of adding up. Infallibly keep at the good
and the good piles up. It's not about trying hard.
It's about allowing laws to operate, art, like fate,

to accumulate, free of the will's distraction.
Strain and stress boomerang fast.
It's a way the universe says:

take it as it comes, and give it back
if you can make it better.

Patience

Biding your time, trusting process, reluctant
to force changes, speed action—impatience being
the very fuel of force—you know you can't force anything

to happen naturally, purely, perfectly, greatly. Just
keep moving through. Flow around impediments.
Love your time. Diligence requires patience,

just like trust and pain. Is it that patience is
the method of all the other virtues? Is it
because patience, while sublimely forceful

never uses force? The impatient can't help
wishing time away, time and the irreplaceable,
the once and only—and only to get what is not quite yet

but will, ever so soon, be what is missed in the next
finger tapping at the oh-so-slowness of the inevitable.

Kindness

Kindness means you see all others as your kind
and treat them kindly as you'd treat yourself,
if you were kind. What matters is that no one

be excluded, dumped into the pit where cruelty
doesn't matter, where you are not them and they are
not you. Being kind and helpful, though, are not the same.

Can we be kind to critters, plants, fast vipers,
weeds, to God and to the gods? Look what happens
if we're not—Auschwitz, the SS, goons who divorce,

as all autocrats do, "wrong" others from their kind.
But be kind to Nazis? What's their overwhelming lesson?
Never, never be unkind, or grand above remorse. But don't

abet them, unless you want the devil of your fears, so eloquent
and doomed, to be your god, your moral force.

Humility

There is no false humility. We never
do anything alone. Even if we dream it up
we don't exactly know where it comes from.

We do know humility is a feeling of the mind
that won't allow us to pretend to be
something other than the dust we are made of,

so we won't deny we are more than the sum
of the miracle of our atoms, more than our flickering
powers. A dead child can't be fixed so its body is

exactly right, and have it come alive again.
Humility is the paradox of being empowered
by being more grateful than powerful.

We'll all be crushed and scattered
if we are powerful and nothing more.

from

Rome MMI
(2015)

I.

Lucretius, physicist of pleasure, coroner of pain,
took the litter down to Herculaneum from Rome
to sun himself in the gardens and to sun his brains
in the libraries of the villa of a Neapolitan epicure
a century or so before the geophysics of Vesuvius
turned the library's scrolls on the peaceful life
to char cased in lava rock and soot, useless
but preserved. There he was before the worst happened,
unworried we suppose, discoursing on the bump
and grind of the atoms while Cicero was trying
to read the tea leaves on Caesar's fortunes
before the Ides of March, breaking Epicurus'
basic rule: flee politics first, don't play the game
of who sticks their neck out the farthest. Rome
was such a hell hole, a volcano seemed safer.

2.

Even after the demolition of centuries, the old pleasures
don't fade, the shadows of the pines, the breezes they bring to the mind,
the sepia shade so pleasing to the inner eye, the egalitarian
joys of Caracalla's propaganda waters free and open to all, now
a stage set for Aida and her snow-white horses, music of the ruins,
far perspectives over the city approachable as the intimate hand
smoothing your back like gliding a palm over polished marble.

3.

Romulus should be the name of the brick, the Temple of Romulus
made of romulus and *pozzolana* unerring regularity, Roman
contracts with eternity cast in cement, a stratigraphy
of conquest, time subdued by lava sand concrete
and the genius to understand that many are stronger than order,
many red layers enduring the sirens of erosion, the power
of accreted growth slow as giant clam shells grow incrusted
layer by impervious layer—imperium—lasting almost forever.

4.

Titus, sacker of Jerusalem, demolisher of the Second Temple,
monster brother of the monster Domitian—time, the alchemist
and artist morphing his triumphal arch into the Arc de Triomphe,
a symbol of Roman infamy digested for the centuries then
        falling out in France
dressed up in the Marseillaise; still tourists see it rising from
        the pines of Rome,
though Titus never walked under his, Hitler did time-warped later
under the replica, and the Free French and de Gaulle himself
        did too after the
Führer's brains were paste on bunker walls.... And now the
        Arch of Titus is prop for
Roman Holidays and Vespas with Rodeo Drive darlings riding
        on the back,
their dark glasses, their curly smiles, their Hollywood knees....

5.

On the Via Sacra, the Hanukkah candelabrum bemedals
the chest of Titus' Arch, like counting coup, a scalp almost
lifted from the corpse of what the menorah's eight-day blaze
celebrates: the spiritual scrubbing-out of the holy space
after the Maccabees drove the Seleucids away 190-odd years
before Titus flattened it. Sacred Ways—they're paved with bones
and chains and rank amnesia, but no stand-up comics
with Jack Benny deadpans gabbing on with shaggy dog
slapstick punch lines about history's exquisite ironies
and dime-a-dozen monuments to the unspeakable.

6.

Temple colonnades, fallen flesh—dreamed up by Greeks,
some say, to mimic sacred groves, with tympanums the shape
of ox hides, in hecatombs, draped to dry over A-frame racks.
Now in Rome, the columns on the ground are more than stone,
they are, if you can see them, petrified forests fallen
in their secondhand history stolen from others
who copied them from trees upside down with roots
as capitals cut from profane woods to simulate
sacred spaces, the lowly become holy when they're dead,
like the names of the fallen no one could remember
when they were living.

7.

Fluted drums, dismembered columns,
dancers broken and strewn on a stage,
skeletons of the temples, tossed on the fine
black wall of time, rising up higher
and higher, shadowing the sun, the flutes themselves
like interiors of bodies you shouldn't see unless
you just couldn't help it, stumbling on what time
had casually turned inside out.

8.

The Medici, Queen Christina, Poussin, Berlioz, Debussy,
the French Academy—only in Rome, the Villa on top
of the Spanish Steps, not far from Keats's digs
and Babington's Tea Room, all in one place, and those pines spying
on the ego-minded, spreading divine breezes over fevered eyes.
Debussy hated Rome, but aside from ghosts, he was, it seems,
very much alone, though Velasquez's view agreed in spirit:
cypress rising behind the villa like on the Isle of the Dead
with its secret melodies, hummed behind hedges by the Finzi-
        Contini;
Respighi's fountains mimicking the Villa's, always playing
The Pines of Rome with water music smooth as heart strings,
startling as tears.

9.

Burt Lahr, Chewbacca, the sadness of the carnivores,
their cosmic grimace—in Rome, or Florence, real or replica,
the Lions of the Medici look out with pained regret upon

the conscience of the universe that must endure the truth
that all living things eat other living things to live themselves.
The sorrow of the flesh-eater might as well be
a monument to the waste of war where meat
is killed but left unchewed, unused, estranged
from the cycles that conscience must accept and must abhor.

10.

That's not a ball of yarn—Lion Colossus, Constellation of the
        Monarchs—
its paw is on the planet, cat toying with the globe—although
noble in his duty, red in tooth and claw, the great gatekeeper
to earthly power, the divine right of felines with big teeth,
is sad to be teasing the world, but loving it to death,

11.

Ten Angels of the Passion, this one with the lance of mercy
that looks to be a lute, "thou hast ravished my heart"
and allowed my body to die. The angels on the Ponte Sant'Angelo,
built by Hadrian over the Tiber, river of corpses
through its Roman course, decades after the Passion,
colonize the bridge of a dead Roman whose state deforested
whole landscapes to crucify the unworthy and troublesome
and the godly, though the emperor himself, with the happy
companionship of his "little soul," restrained the cruelty
of power just enough so that his Mausoleum will always
have the magnanimous grace of a pagan's welcoming
from angels of the firmament—all the gods, or none.

12.

Here on the ponte where the bodies of the executed
jutted out unangelic into the air above the renaissance river,
here the angel of the Passion sings "upon my vesture
they cast lots,"—it has always been a gamble in Rome
to be a full human being. Bruno, down the way
in the flower stalls cleared off for his stake and pyre,
couldn't lie to save his hide, his vesture of skin,
the life of his mind, a terrible gamble, had proved to him
the divine is both in us and beyond us, quite apart
from the endless dice game of time. If ideas
were flammable, I'd have burned up with him.

13.

Bernini's shy angelic girl, a glory of wings—her wistful sorrow
and abasing joy, she who sings that "God has reigned
from the tree." Rome has always arisen and sunk back
into its clotted mess and backup from cloacae, the carnaria
with black ooze from centuries of circuses, and now,
beneath its streets, the albino joint bones of its early selves
stack up all the way down even unto the very beginning.
Rising up. Rising up. In Santa Maria del Popolo,
Jesus leaps from the cross while the Church puts a lid
on contemplation but never on His jubilant abandonment
of the nails of politics, clanking to the marble floor.

from

Memoirs of the World

(2018)

Preface

EVERYONE'S LIFE IS INTERESTING in some particular way because each of us is a representative of the species, ordinary and remarkable at the same time. And each of us is, of course, a unique and irreplaceable person living in a specific place that has, as its context, the entirety of existence as it moves through time at a specific moment in the flow of history. As a writer born in 1940, I realized when I turned seventy that what is most interesting to me about my specific life is what I have witnessed of my imagination in my practice as a poet, what I have witnessed of the world as a journalist and nonfiction writer, and what I have witnessed of the will to love and the will to destroy. This is not to say that I am uninterested in the details of my life. But my self-interest is interwoven with the magnetism of life as it exists moment to moment on the planet in unique and universal ways.

I am drawn to history because it is at once a conglomeration of fact and a realm of the imaginary built of anecdotes which are stories of the truth, if not the truth itself, that bear no resemblance to mere abstractions like statistics. It came to me that if I were to do a memoir late in life I would like it to be a memoir of the world. My task would be to write poems through the lens of my personality as a witness to the contents of my own awareness. A memoir of the world would have to be immediate, fragmentary, and subliminally "occasional." So I opened myself up and started writing every day for more than four years on what came my way through this focus. I found myself expressing over and over an astonishment at the simultaneity of everything—the beautiful and horrific, the merciful and cruel, the stupid, kind, sadistic, the selfless, the maniacal, the naïve—everything all at once, everywhere in world, most often with no apparent meaning or regularity and usually with alarming speed and reversals. It's never seemed to me that the world is intent on going somewhere, nor has it seemed that its apparent randomness is without purpose or meaning—both of which are, apparently, beyond our intelligence to grasp.

When I turned my attention to taking seriously what my experience was revealing to me I saw the overwhelming confusion most of us find impossible to live with for long, a confusion of reality that forces us to invent versions of truth that we can bear. It's not too much to say that the great tragedy of the world's memoirs is not that it's physically beyond anyone's ability to write anything more than the barest fragments, but that a whole reality of an alternative world made up of the interior, invisible, and largely inexpressible private selves of the billions of human lives that have experienced the world so far is literally a profound existence that simply does not exist beyond the confines of the skull. The quantum of the personal self, not to mention the inconceivable treasure of the flow of human conversation, does not register even the faintest ripple in the gravity of history. We are, but we are not. How can any of us be known if we hardly know ourselves, glimpsing only an albedo of our inner selves and personal cultures? We are, like dry leaves, potential humus. Our appearance in the lives of others is dependent on memory, which is as substantial, one might say, as all the last breaths ever taken.

When modern physicists like Stephen Hawking talk about the "multiverse," a cosmos of infinite universes in a "superposition of states," they are speaking as well of the tiny world in which we exist in time and space, a world in which everything happens all at once, in a sequence everywhere we can never quite grasp. Time is the common ground, space is the idiosyncratic. But it is a sure bet that what's happened over there to them has a chance of happening to us over here. Not that it will, but that it can, with no doubt. The only questions, locked in time and chance, are which and when and if.

Realizing the inadequacy of these memoirs, I offer them nonetheless as a token sacrifice to the Gods of the Inexplicable in thanks for the life they have allowed me to lead so far, one in which I escaped dire poverty and emotional abuse to find myself momentarily fumbling with magical privilege in the cold shadow of celebrity and then, by the roulette of off-the-cuff choices, rooting myself in the outback of New Mexico, falling into poverty again, working my way out, and then marrying the best person I have ever known, the artist Rini Price, and being graced with wonderful children and grandchildren and with the luck to spend more than fifty years laboring at what I love, writing and editing, studying and teaching. I have led the secret life of people who make new things, the sources of which are as mysterious as our dreams and leave us with the inescapable feeling that there is more going on behind appearances, even our own, than we are apparently equipped to perceive or give form to through reason.

Who can believe the world is as it is?

In Utah Canyonlands, at Needles Overlook, the Divine is clearer
  in its morality than it ever is
  passing through words;
morality in change, in stone, wind, soil, water,
  in what gives way, what stays in the perfect now,
so much more precise than books, than neurons and their
   social subtlety,
  their white glove, tiara, cummerbund restraints,
  Corporal Hitler shoveling snow, hating the the rich
   stepping into the golden warmth
  of the Berlin Opera

Moral books of murderous, jealous, tyrant gods, Machiavellian
  snickerers who translators have all confused with kings
and lesser monsters of the midway

The unseen moving through
the spontaneous being of the world, allowing the old
  street magician to be a lazy genius, allowing all the love
  you couldn't help, the long disasters, lost peace
  in the magic of plenty

Reading the papers over supper under soft lights in the perfect
  luxury of being safe
  in a restaurant patio on a summer night, paranoia,
   crumpling stress,
  even news panics
beyond adrenaline's reach

Students rising to their reality with the merest
    touch of interest, going to their depths
    so the singular
rushes from them like sweet cold from a melon

Conveyor belt industrial death by machine tool philosophies of
    worthlessness and value

Abandoned, a derelict on Christmas eve, all delight
    deflated. The world so cold, war seemed like warmth.
Then at someone's door, appearing from the snow, she handed
    him a paper sack.
"Here's a miracle," she said. He reached inside
    and lifted out a rough, round stone, bigger than his hand.
"It's a geode. Crack it open."
The hammer stuck the surface several times and then
    the puzzling hard gray circle fell away and there:
an astonishing, wild radiant surprise, a crystal cave, a star change
    like the greatest kindness of our lives.
It came to stand for all
    that we don't know. To be alive,
    the beauty's mostly hidden till you find it.

Weather drowning millions, movies diverting millions from
    moments of truth,
the arts of great cultures
    celebrating glory,
        painting food and sweet garden life
while others eat dirt and die on water so soiled
they could have almost grown food in it,
    if it weren't for the solvents

Where each self exists embedded
    in a world of other selves—the furies of their pettiness,
      their judicious
    hates and disappointments, their overwhelming
    joy in chocolates and all else
      that seems to their cells
    like now
    is long, long ago when purity was not
    ever to be questioned
—selves that make a mire of the sunshine live in makebelieves
    they can't escape

This world where people lose their jobs and lose their homes
    and lose their lives
    because they were merely unlucky

Beaches so pure and safe some children can grow golden on
    them without a care

La Mer on the refugee boat hobbled by wolf packs just evaded,
Mozart trailing technicians of torture on their daily rounds,
Beethoven coexisting in a world of mountain tops leveled for
    copper and coal

Where vast industries mulch trees to make books that save
    people's lives, save their sanity, give
    them hope for the best, millions of times a day

Miners trapped so far underground their deaths won't even
    make good humus

Where ego turns against the egoist, were humility is always
      left behind in the dust
    without the ego fighting for every inch,
where timidity and caution are disguised as one another in
      their naked slowness, where wanting
    it too much
    makes you lose it,
where not wanting at all
    is a blank

Conquerors taking what's yours, everything you've made,
      everything you cherish because they
    want to and you can't stop their wanting
    even when you survive them

Christmas mornings, nylon stockings filled with presents, Mother
more sober with maternal joy
than I am joyous—happy as I am to know how the day will go,
      how it "always" goes
    when sacred sentiment rules and I'm distracted by the
    presents
replacing food next week

Rachmaninov's Russian blues pouring through rainy dumps of
      European streets slick with
    rainbow oil and ghosts of millions decomposing in the
    undermind,
poison enigmas, strangled joy

Pacific coast cafes, wave safe, windy, salt cold midnight, inside
steamy light, coffee, hot cakes, bacon, maple syrup and
          phenomenology
     pencil underlined in erotic struggles for complicity to
     understand

Dingy cities with great boulevards and down at the heel genius
          neighborhood men
     dejected sitting on sidewalks waiting for coin and the
     alchemy of metal into food as you
     walk by, feet too sore for you to think
to find some random change until you're too far past to turn
     and find
     you have to change to make a change

A whole frame of mind—a political dog-chew-dog mind—a mind
          with big teeth and big bucks
     that just doesn't like old people, poor people, ill people,
     children in trouble, gay people,
     the infirm, the mad, the immobilized depressed. Some put
     them in trucks with hoses in
     the windows attached to the tailpipes and kill them off
     without apology, some bully haters just write laws to
     grave-dig the impoverished farther down out of sight to
     save themselves a
     penny. Who do they like? The rich beyond care, like
     themselves

Midnight earthquakes infusing dreams with confusions and
          suffocations, monsoons drowning
     villages, walls of mud, last gasps inhaling caliche,

pregnant mothers breathing aerosol nukes from DU rounds
     haunting old war zones with killing
    dust coating cars and babies
tornadoes tossing neighborhoods into the air, lumber and glass
     and furnishings like the leavings
    scattered on ant piles

Where runes and gods and stone circles and meteors form
     meaning
as real to us as oxygen and photons are invisible, as weather
     and the flesh cannot be missed,
     meaning from endless layers
     of magical
     association, the pen point found in the gutter with which
     he wrote
everything because of its holy
unlikelihood

Men and women stolen from their lives, chained in slave ships,
     packed fish in tins,
     claustrophobic mayhem maddening them for weeks on
     high seas, released into a world
     wild with pain in which they exist to function and nothing
     more

Painters who transform flowers into feelings, lines and edges
     into sensations, graphite into reality
     as delicate and refined as retinas themselves, making
     things of color-form that transcend
     themselves, that are optical wind sounds in trees and
     grass irresistible as pearls or the
     inner snow curve of a thigh

Rooms full of rich sophisticates tearing up at musicians barely
        keeping their families fed playing
        music by often tortured souls who put symphonies to
        storms of clouds rolling off the
        tops of imaginary Himalayas

Sioux women, granddaughters of far roamers, starving in
        Budweiser hovels on Rosebud and
        Pine Ridge gulags,
men who would once cut off a finger to coax god's voices, falling
        in the snow stupefied to seem
        like Wounded Knee corpses frozen in booze and ice

Recluse's writing as Orpheus sings himself back from the dead
        through everyone,
        our voices praising breath through speech that means
life is not death, and the yellow of the woman's robe in the
        painting is as
        cosmic-absolute a yellow as the yellow on a sea shell

Gardens in the city where Pan wears shorts and plays in the
        sandbox of the universe as flowers
        bloom mechanically, teasing bees and intoxicating the
        financially blessed
in the early morning sanctity of their enclosures beyond the
        streets, the thieves and corrupt police

How is it possible this life has come to be as it is?

Sadness soft as hot down pillows pulled from under your head
        and held against your face

Waiting for something to happen, for the world to take shape
        around us when it must take shape
        within us and from us

A world of facades and accidents where a person can invent
        other worlds in rooms of two-by-fours, pink insulation,
        wall board and stucco not a full foot
        from the street
and never know the traffic flow, the cold, the bitter light while
        living in a bathrobe truth amid
        books and rocks and knowledges that could be dismissed
as fast as a cyclone moving through an oil patch trailer park

Firestorming generals pronouncing bombers "the most humane
        of all weapons," while patriot
        editors rhapsodize that "Japanese cities will burn like
        autumn leaves"

Rescued by a woman with a glass heart so hard it would
        survive an oven,
a woman who wanted the best, who wanted family, who
        wanted beauty and loved to look perfect
        as a set on a sound stage, genuine
        feelings made to feel safe as window dressings with fine
        decor and the kind of food that
        looks so good
love might have made it

Loved by a mother so beset with grief, so traumatized by her
        father, so heartbroken
        by her worshipped husband's lack of love for her, she
        abandons the child she adores
        to gin

A world where you can
survive your delusions, your illusions, your fixations, your
      compulsions, even your minor addictions and all your
      catastrophic loves, your pushings of the possible beyond,
and emerge
capable, accomplished and in love
all the way
with someone who loves you all the way, luck holding true
     while running out
     now and then, recharging, and then
some splinter of an accident, some frail, almost invisible touch
    of the devil
     sends luck into remission
like an infected finger
loses an arm

Mentored by a father who loved the world, worshiped the
     miracles of matter and neurology,
    and was a widespread
disappointment to himself, who escaped it all on the road
selling small-town culturati on the gravity and joy of art
and its double appreciation

And me, blessed with unnatural optimism, privileged
with experience, covered in love right or wrong,
someone, it turns out, who has to know every thing terrible
    about humankind, so he can
forebear with himself, knowing the deep worst of darkness and
    folly

A world in which it is possible to destroy
whole species, millions of years
  of evolutionary proof
   in the blink of a quarterly report, where mafias, pirates,
    drug lords, the CEOs of the great
   corporations will slaughter
   innocent hope for an uptick of the Dow
and a notch on the six shooter of Cold Warrior Dominos and
    other games of chance and
   genocide

A child who was given the ocean, kidnapped by love to a soda
    shop with his magical mother, who sniffed crumb cake
    on the windowsill of his foster mother, who knew adults
   who had lived through the normalcy
  of madness in a world that lived
  on fantasy and facade

Who knew Mexico City like the soft taste of her mouth,
who saw his father hanged in the movies, who went from insane
poverty at fourteen, life on a boozer's budget, to a sumptuous world
all for show, who was
   around it, but couldn't have much of it,
as the adults spoiled themselves while not spoiling him

A world of horrors where the brave die fast, the fearful
suffer through life as if
it were a lingering death, where the cruel laugh at the pain
   of others, beg for mercy
when their nature turns against them,
   a bigger beast chewing
   their heads very slowly

Who saw his heroes die
of their virtue;
the wise, happily round, stubborn old woman whose dignity,
        independence, and no fuss
        brilliance in the world, whose utterly tidy card tables
            with their perfect papers and that
        perfect pen,
dissolved into a long, emaciating refusal,
shrinking her into the grave of no-fuss, no-muss, no-
        matter depression until she vanished
            altogether under the linens
after decades of shrinking and bewildered, mute sadness

Where fear of mind freezing up freezes mind to a blankness which
        refreezes and seizes until you forget
how afraid you are of forgetting, and what
that might mean,
and you remember your memory all your life and know how
        faulty it's always been and given to
        freezing, then and now—such is the warmth and looseness
        of fact

Dead friends littering the past, live friends like grapes
        on the vine, and me
who married the goddess of all goodness and joy, and never let go,
        even when life was trying to
        take itself away from her, even then, when all the irony of
        his past seemed like a knife at
        her throat and in his craw

Meditating in Santa Maria del Popolo, free of panic at last,
      rising to meet the heartbeat of the
         gods in their cosmic harmony, spirit lifting up—and then
           the heavenly ceiling and its
         cherubim, then
bump,
      then stop, then contained, imprisoned, limited, oh
so this is what the devil is all about. Put a lid on it!
More faggots on Bruno's fire!

Tut from Alabama, trench war doughboy, gardener, patron of
      the lonely and afraid, Miss Eedieth
         and her Spare Ribs boy, great spirit of the gentle laugh,
           the slow joke on himself, the
         effortless will to be kind so deeply in him, Jim Crow could
           do his worst
and never fix his teeth or touch his grin and soft, slow melting
         smile

Where fear and uncertainty are more binding than fifty-ton
      boulders falling
         on your car,
where microchips work magic so small they seem like god's
         secrets, where meteors and mind-made bombs can
           obliterate the million minds of libraries in the twinkling
           of a morning,
a world of race hate, sex hate, and
         forgiving, forbearing, merciful doubt

Learning to read the Korean War with the L.A. *Times* at ten,
      horrified and mesmerized, headlines
         blaring war games in ice and snow with real blood and
         men who would hate you to death; words hurt like
         reality, when you can't stop reading

Desk sanctuaries, secret islands, camps all our own; we're all
        Robinson Crusoe
    when it comes to being stranded on imagination's blotter,
        its higher plane;
we must learn
    the lay of the surface, find control there at least,
        surrounded by icons, tools, magic
    stones and equipment, the contents of other minds
        pressed in old bound paper
cherished as the favorite shirt you were sure made you seem
as handsome as you really were

Where the now, right now, the nano now is all that's safe
        and all that's free, and nothing else
    is dependable but
    the vanishing, non-existent now

Beloved old friends who you no longer console or excuse;
        the exuberant intoxicant, popsicle
    prince, who asked "Are you a wizard or a magician?"
        who took down a walker in the
    dusk, hit and run, ruined a life, drunk to the nines,
        his guilt the key to the dungeon of his
    death
sighing in relief alone

Six-year-old waterwinging near Diamond Head, father on a
        court-ordered flight across the high
    seas, and me too afraid to spend the night alone in palm
        groves while he scintillates in
    Trader Vic's till my wailing brings him back to rescue me
        from another
grand fiasco of abandonment

Two thousand sailors drowning in flaming metal coffins, an
      infamy six years and not two miles
    away from Waikiki

Creating personas to survive behind, the sophistication of
      cigarette smoke, the frown to put
        wrinkles into a sixteen-year-old face while shopping for
        Christmas gifts for his nobility,
        wearing long-gone father's shirts and coats, his ties and
        handkerchieves;
passing in Montana and Wyoming with my own
awful perfect old Wrangler ball cap soiled by years of travel
      with imagination's joyheart, sweeter
    than all the hawks and swallows, all
    the far wind rivers, all the wild horses staring at you
    though dust and the tall grass by the
    road

The stroke friend, the cancer old comrade, the heart attack
      epileptic collapsed alone on the floor,
        the guilt-vice squeezing the facile drinker's head till his
        esophagus explodes
    and drowns him in his own bloody blood

Where the gods actually do intercede, and worship, devotion,
      sincerity in thanks really do
        mean the difference, when you ask and receive and live as
        you've been told by the voice
    of Kindness
    inside you, when you know
    no success is yours but the wild truth of the cosmic good
      working through you, despite
    you, over and around you, giving and giving until you stoop
    to take credit
and it all turns into snake skins fluttering through the grasses

Lynching, gassing, shooting, frying, and all the other
          unmentionable brutalities we visit upon the
     convicted while sausages are being stuffed and socks
          darned and sails mended,
     and perfect white collars starched and ironed, and Fall
          gardens planted with garlic and
     shallots in compost lovingly tended for a year

Beds, so soft and warm the kings of a thousand years would
          have traded their scepters for one
     of them and viciously kept the rabble sleeping on stones,
          in shit, too hungry to think of
     the cave hollowing out their intestines
as they digest themselves with minor satisfaction

Where immortal gods have been known to die, gods that
          condemned disbelievers to everlasting
     fire, deranging their lives, gods who just went puff and
          the fires along with them

Where life gives murderous dilemmas, catching us between
          love's multiple jaws, forcing us to
     choose between them
     and when we can't
forcing us to choose against ourselves with fatal illness
          as the only way out

Photographs of the slaughtered, of movie-star weddings, of
          buildings moth-eaten by howitzers, authors signing
          their books with suspicious grins, the executed bleeding
          in the streets, black
     coffee in little white cups, tyrants tearing up as they
          board the plane to delicious exile,

miners smiling on the way out and up to supper, lumberjacks
        warming up smoking, a cat
      splashing though wind over a Viennese gutter, the famous
        looking their parts

Each of us, in the same world,
each just another life
living to see
how it all turns out.

Reading in a big chair in the morning when the day seems
auspicious, hot coffee, pillows, pencils, all the miracles
        of the goddess
of comforts yours.

The foot was broken in three places, but he had to do his chores
        or not get paid.

She was kind and loving to everyone, many loved her back,
        but not in the way she wanted.

His childhood was the apogee. He died happy to be done with it.

A scholar explains to an old student why Lucretius
gave Bruno his fire and why it set him aflame.

The latest sucker from the current bush aspires
to height and dark foliage. He waters it thinking
of his old friend who died but who used to
win every time at the standing hop step and jump
in the driveway at birthday parties long ago
when family meant something to everyone, even
the recently adopted, or especially them.

Her old age sang with contentment. She never thought her luck
    would change.

The gang of two took the Studebaker's engine apart
and put it back together again in a father's garage.
They had three parts left over when they were done.
The car started. Then stopped for good.

As he was planting tomatoes in New Mexico a farmer in
    Cambodia
was smothered to death with a plastic grocery bag over his
    head by an ideological child of ten.

Pelicans swooped in squadrons close to the waves, wave after
    wave of them.

Her hand reached for his... they sang the little song, jolly
    friends forevermore... the elm trees' dark green
    welcoming shadows on the ditch.

Who can believe the world is as it is?

Christmas Poems
(2018-2020)

Five Treasure Maps to the Labyrinth of Trust

Map Number One: Knowing What You Know

That's the vine tossed to you in the quicksand of self-pity
as you tread suction in a morass of laughs.
That kind of knowledge comes from having a feel
    for the invisible. The palm-sized crystal globe
    shows more than a circle. It lets you know,
    with your own eyes, the inside is real
even if you can't see all of it. So what do you trust?

You are certain you exist, even if you must
    doubt your certainty. You know for sure
    you don't know enough. You know the cosmos
    cannot be some sick joke played on the sentient
by a ludicrous devil god anymore than it can be
    a passing thought in the Mind of the Divine. Or can it?
    You know that love is the only thing that bears

no possibility of guilt, in itself. You know when you are lost.
You know the invisible is the way the mystery appears,
as when a living thing dies, it's merely a pile of parts
    no science can revive. You know that kindness is right
    and cruelty is wrong, that love is the truth.
    You know, it turns out, quite a lot.
But can you find your way out?

Map Number Two: Doubt as Evidence

Doubt is the flying trapeze between
    what you think you know and what actually is.
It's the best way across and it's always without a net.
Losing your way is not a tragic circus act, if you make the catch.
    It leads to getting found, to finding out
for yourself how to fly, free of delusions of grace. Even if
    the scalpel of doubt is sharpened

only to butter-knife standards, it can still slice
    though the stink of hate. When something
doesn't add up, like saying a puma skull is where
all its catness lay, as if a cat was invulnerable to its prey,
    or when a specialist generalizes absolute truth
we take that as a ludicrous self-deception,
    malign balderdash. We leave the room

when a poppycock general, protesting goodness too much,
    tries to make us doubt what doubt has taught us.
Doubt too much, not too little. But never doubt
the paradoxes that do you in. Doubt doubts itself.
    You can trust it until it becomes your standard response.
Then unlock the cage, and let it flap and growl its way
    over the labyrinth and escape all the rules.

Map Number Three: Revulsion and Attraction

It is not up to us, our gag reflex can't be denied.
We can't swallow political maggots
or swindling rats in our food. We can't stomach sadism,
    hate rancid propaganda. Revulsion is a faultless map.
    Attraction starts the same, it's just easier to lose your way
than it is to be found. That dinosaur turd of your dad's,
    it looks like it's wet and stinks, but when you touch it

    it's a stone, a coprolite, an object of abject fascination
    to a child, shit keeping its form for millions of years.
When repulsed you flee. The doctor who labels you at a glance
    and treats you like a quick description,
    shun him like you would a dinosaur shitting.
With attraction, if you trust the gravity of it, the helplessness
    of its powers, being pulled inexorably,

    then attraction is as grave as falling. It goads possession,
    the old slapstick of confusing having with being.
You must see if who you are attracted to is attracted to you,
    what kind of closeness is compelled.
    You trust it, how could you not? It is gravity after all.
But to be safe you must wait in the maze to see how fast
    empathy finds the pathway too, and if it's looking for you.

Map Number Four: Intuiting Up and Down

High-wire dancing, the inner gyroscope cuts you no slack,
reveals time's razor line getting lost in plain sight.
        You can feel life and death with the soles of your feet.
        But vertigo sets in. Something's taking you under,
a riptide of more than depression—and it comes to you
that this down is dangerous and that the bottom
        is too far down. You must stop minding. It's not unlike

trusting your fathomless sadness sinks with perpetual fear
coming true in the end, fear the clairvoyant, like a shark
        as a chaperone, thrashing at the bottom, not knowing
        up from down. When it comes to survival,
you don't need hard evidence. Like when you're told
thought is a sparkling secretion and love a tango of molecules,
        not metaphorically, but neurologically for real,

you sense the powerful have purged doubt from themselves.
You are your own seeing-eye dog.
        You know that intuition is
        catching the right scent among the millions
of stray aromas—hey, there's a bear right around the corner,
over there an angel is just about to tell you sweetly what not to do.
        That you can take into battle.

Map Number Five: Love as Gravity

Love is unquestioned, undoubted, irrefutable.
It is losing the way to being lost. It has no opposite.
It trusts you to be who you are. Hate is not on its spectrum.
Standing on the rim of the Milky Way, or the precipice
    before the fossil sea bed of canyons and spires,
    seeing your grandchildren smile, the warm eyes
of your lover, she whose love was the equal sign

    that joined the best of you to the rest of everything—
    those are maps that *are* the territory just as being
bowled over by Bach in the garden is, or holding the stone
with stratigraphy of eons in the palm of your hand,
    as is your admiration of time and what it makes—
    the 300-million-year-old seashell replaced
with fool's gold so precise and perfect without intent,

    it makes you laugh with longing. So many
    treasure maps to the sublime. The labyrinth of trust
ends and begins by looking yourself straight in the eye.
Like finally being allowed to speak her native tongue,
    the connoisseur of clouds cannot help but find herself
    in love with the goodness that made her know
that any love is good.

(2018)

Five Innocent Merriments
of Being in Love Again with Being Alive

1. Dancing with Time

Entropy dismantles everything. Nothing is spared,
vibrant life or crooked malice. Our homes
run down, so does our despair and the intolerable
sufferings of fear. Confidence wanes and joy
can play itself out, but so does terror, exquisite pain.
The single truth that change never touches,
until it's all over, is the mystery of
perpetual emotion, the spontaneous new,
infinite jolt of falling in love with being alive.
Even entropy itself runs out of gas. Only
the gravity of love changes without
diminishment as the everlasting source

of goodness that entropy clears the way
to refresh, again and again, never ceasing.

II. It Loves You Back

When you fall in love with being alive,
life loves you back. What doesn't love
to be loved? What doesn't feel humbled
and ecstatic with the luck of not being left
unrequited? Love the sun and it lets you see
its green and growing edge moving through
the darkest human history like a forest moves
renewed across an ashen void. Falling in love
smooths flaws, sees genius in oddity, morphs
blemishes and bulges into sweet slopes and curves,
restores trust and withers grudges with just
the fascination, the single focus

of adoring curiosity. And life itself
always knows it, and gives you back all it's got.

III. Not a Sick Joke

So many two-by-fours careening through the fog of chance
—is this a cosmic sick joke played out in the rumpus
room galaxy of an infernal brat? It's not credible
that the entirety of it all is a prank and the mind
a shaggy dog story with homicidal malice.
It just doesn't compute. Is it all without value
when the cosmos creates in us the expectation
of value? Focus, she always said, on what
doesn't hurt. Forbear, adore, fall in love
and you will see all the rest, what's not
disordered, like you would see your child,
your lover, the mountains, a stormy sky,

see the cosmos like that, as a cherished soul
not a perverse, random and vindictive pest.

IV. Too Beautiful to Resist

Dawn light opalized through mountain cold,
how can you resist the bare beauty of the world
once you see it, once you know it will be everywhere
you choose to look, if you choose to look? How can you
resist falling in love with everything
beautiful and kind, compassionate in its strength,
how can you resist touching the smooth,
long flow of time as if it were warm sea foam
around your ankles, or over there, running
through the meadow, shooting stars
invisible around her, daughter of the weather,
grand in her childhood and in her blood bond

with you, the gift of generations—how can you resist
falling in love again with being alive?

V. Splendor, Mirth, and Good Cheer

Being in love, we can see the truth of life
for what it is as it happens. Imperfection, pain,
blindsiding bad luck, all exist in spacetime
as fun does, as flesh-and-blood hope,
mirth, and quanta darting and effervescing do.
It's all inconceivably pointless and purposeful
without end. Is pain more powerful than humor?
Is irony more truthful than skin-and-bone love?
If misery is more convincing than warm breezes,
of course suicide is the only rebuttal. But add up
the totals. Cruelty and evil exist. They are random
shrapnel shredding peace for a while, but are not

equal in power to the gentleness they disquiet
as they vanish passing through.

(2019)

Travel Notes on Coming Back to Life
In Memoriam: Rini Price

WAKING UP,
plucked from the void, a new
stretch of mind, all yours
to fill, all yours, and already
partially behind you, the only
actual possession you have:
the world moving through you.

COMING BACK TO LIFE,
you might feel
the full
dark
miracle,
magnificent
with galaxies,
geodes, a chambered nautilus,
jellyfish, island forests,
mountain snow
and goldfinches in the thorns.
And you want
all the gifts, all of them
you never knew were given
until death dumped you
awake again
to everything
you'd thought
nothing of
before.

TIME FOLDS ITSELF UP.
You can't unfold it
without tearing it apart.
Never forget
what it might mean
to be dead.

YOU KISSED HER FOREHEAD,
you said the love charms
in her ear, you looked upon
her eyelids, shut so tight,
not sunken yet, but soon,
yellow and dark, as if her eyes,
once flowers of light,
were withering in the cold
blank tunnel of her dying.

SUPPOSE YOUR HEART STOPS,
you're unaccountably blank,
blank to the world, blank
to yourself, but then
you're plucked, like a kid
from a riptide, alive,
no longer blank, like the day
when death, present
as ever, strummed your ear
while you were kissing and said
"live, I am coming."

LET'S SAY THAT HAPPENED,
a Lazarus tale,
arising, without
any memory
of being gone,
life dawning
on you again.
What does it mean?
It wasn't a long
trip into the zero.
I didn't slide for hours
through ice sheets
of foggy eyes.
I didn't encounter
the rose of light
at the center of heaven.
I slipped in and out
in a flash of darkness,
an anomaly,
a fatal stubbing
of the toe, but not.

JUST BEING AWAKE
in the world of trees,
of brains alive,
of war and pain,
of mulberries
and lawns
of flax and Maximilians,
just being awake

opens it *all*,
all of it
available
for *you*, all of it,
however
much of it
you can stand.

YOU KNOW THAT ANY LIFE
can stop at any second. It's a knowing
that doesn't make you more alive,
with a keener sense of danger,
but you do get better at tightrope-walking
over the abyss on a sunny day
barefoot on a soggy rope. That's where
all the best dancing you have to give
has to be done, simple as breathing
"thank you, thank you, thank you" forever
into the empty yawning of what was once
the solace of your shameful boredom.

THE MORNING RESSURECTION
is true. This everyday
reappearance on the stage
of the way the world is,
this is our life as it is lived
before it is over, before there is an after
to all our losses, all our exiles, before we can regret
having been too stingy to pay attention before our life
is threatened with its end
that just happens
like anything else.

LIFE SPREADS OUT BEFORE US,
the whole realm of being.
It's all here in all its ways
and always will be
until the body leaves
and takes us with it.
Each time we die
to our fears, die
to our doubts, die
to our shabby indifference,
life takes us over, fills us
with everything,
edge to edge, like light
takes up the sky.

We know. Don't
waste a moment.
Death is always
a moment too soon.

(2020)

Jupiter and Saturn
For Robin

Just like that
the Solstice saw, exactly

without dogma,
Jupiter and Saturn smooth

together through
deep space last night,

the light fantastic
in syncopation as

a single star, binary as
our inspired conversation

of touch and word, moving
through the arbitrary night

together, regular as breathing.
It wasn't that we'd glanced

over our shoulders and beheld
Venus as the morning star

and felt the suffering
of our world all fall away.

It was us,
that's all,

as perfect
as your hand

in mine,
my old life all yours;

your exquisite, wise,
brave loving

and overcoming
warming me to take

devoted gambles,
to risk joy

as if it were
as simple as

turning to face
delicious breezes

out back in the summer
near the corn and beans.

We are now how
each of our lives

has unfolded.
We are what's next,

star paths joined
on the dark waters

of our histories,
a singular amazement

woven though
the tapestries

of our terrible
dread chances,

each of us now
wild rivers of light

flowing through
the constellation

of our trust that is
as regular as it has

become a parallel that
liberates and guides,

and gives the night of the world
clear meaning,

warm as coming home
to find your shoes

left easy on
the bedroom floor

while you
were changing for

a Boxing Day
in calm abandon.

That's the peace
you give me, lyrical

as you dancing barefoot
in the kitchen

with a band
of pots and pans,

your exquisite
care and taste

smoothing into
sweet hilarities

that trust has made
as safe as light

that has no shadow.
And so we know

laughter-loving Aphrodite
always shows the way

to walk on water
though the din of fate,

the whirring two-by-fours
and us

braving history now
together as a miracle

illumined as the gravity
two stars have made

across dark waters
side by side, a path,

a chance impossible
and sweeter by far

than all lost luck
was ever cruel,

all ours now,
singular and duel

as the two of us are
simple as trust

turned into touch,
a matter of fact,

unique and parallel,
regular and true.

UNTAMED AS LIGHT,
de-lightful in fact,

de-lighted, as we are
with light flooding

our Elysium, the body
that has suffered so

many deaths around us is,
now, our field of joy again,

our paradise, living to the last
full inch and breath

of what we're given—feral
as the world is feral,

hair-raisingly free to be
so happy to touch and watch

ecstasy flower like the sun
finally reaching the shadowed side

of the canyon where we longed
and waited faithfully for morning heat,

for the edge of night to just move up
and away, sunlight washing

the chill and sadness from our grasp,
our hands clean of the future

which has become, because of us,
the living, quick and warming now.

SHE EMBODIES
a bond that cannot break,

a principle of trust
that makes all honesty

possible and without which
all candor fails

and becomes paradoxical
in its intent, causing

tragedies of confession,
burdening and self-serving,

not a longing to say the
loving truth, not a closeness but

a shabby coupe of ego, an exploitation
of kind listening. Her wise caring,

now, for me, a deep sounding
in the fathomless light-

hearted truth of Venus
the Joyous, the only

rock to build a life on,
the only sand to fill and heal

the cracks and chasms
of old oversights, sleights

of inattention and tiny foolish
histories of the obstacles of fear.

Rock and sand, love's all-
encompassing geography,

global, intimate, an Eden
unbounded, a sweet tangle of fun,

naked of pretense, the only boundary
one plus one, the singularity of two.

(2020)

Acknowledgments

I AM DEEPLY GRATEFUL to Zach Hively—publisher, editor, designer, shipping clerk, and everything else at Casa Urraca Press near Abiquiu, New Mexico—for making this book possible. These poems would probably have never been gathered together without his overall understanding of the direction of the work I've been doing as poet. His great artistry as a book designer gives clarity to the various interlocking suites of poems that I've worked on since 2008. I've been blessed over the years with superb editors: Roland Dickey, Beth Hadas, and Luther Wilson at UNM Press, Mark Acuff at the New Mexico *Independent*, Jack Ehn the Editorial Page Editor of the Albuquerque *Tribune*, Bryce Milligan of Wings Press, Benito Aragon of the New Mexico *Mercury* and *Mercury Messenger*, and now Zach Hively of Casa Urraca Press. They've all helped me be the best that I can be on the page.

My heartfelt thanks go to Bryce for taking a chance with publishing a beautifully designed edition of a long poem sequence of mine called *Memoirs of the World in Ten Fragments*. My association with writer, editor, and designer Benito Aragon has been one of the great good fortunes of my writing life. Our years of friendship and editorial collaboration in the dicey world of online publishing have kept me going as a columnist since the *Tribune* folded in 2008. With almost no money at all, Benito, with a little help from me, published and edited an elegant online weekly called the New Mexico *Mercury* for the better part of four years. We published more than two hundred authors and poets. His technical knowledge, editorial range, and aesthetic sensitivity make him the best collaborator one could have.

I've been blessed as well with the friendship of writer Margaret Randall and artist Barbara Byers, and their ongoing miraculous productivity. Margaret and Barbara have heard the first draft and later drafts of virtually every poem I've written in the last decade or more. Hearing my own work in their presence has become a touchstone experience of trust and creative candor.

My life could have been fatally diminished without the fifty-two years of love and support of my late wife Rini Price, and the generous wisdom of my confidant and new life partner Robin Swift. Robin and I share a home in Albuquerque's North Valley called El Rancho Puerco Volador, the Flying Pig Ranch, because the vast and miraculous good fortune of meeting each other sums up the meaning of that exclamation: It'll happen when pigs fly!

About the author

V. B. PRICE HAS BEEN WORKING to repair his ignorance since he came to New Mexico in 1958 at the age of eighteen. He studied anthropology and philosophy at the University of New Mexico and has been publishing poetry since 1962. He's worked continuously as a reporter and an environmental and political columnist for nearly as long. His column currently runs weekly at mercmessenger.com. He had the great privilege of teaching at UNM's School of Architecture and Planning and in UNM's Honors College for more than three decades. His books include *Innocence Regained: Christmas Poems, Chaco Trilogy, Memoirs of the World in Ten Fragments, The Orphaned Land: New Mexico's Environment since the Manhattan Project, Mythwaking, The Seven Deadly Sins*, and *Albuquerque: A City at the End of the World*. He recently received the 2021 New Mexico Literary Arts Gratitude Award for contributions to the life of the poetry community in New Mexico and the Southwest, and he has also been elected to the Board of Directors for the Leopold Writing Program.

His father once called him "fortune's child." The vast luck of his life is embodied in his children, his grandchildren, and in the landscape of his beloveds both in the ground and still walking upon it. His good fortune blossoms in the students who have mentored him, the friends who have taught him, and in New Mexico who has mothered him.

Casa Urraca Press

WE ARE A HOME for words that speak to the soul and stimulate thought. We publish daring, eloquent authors of poetry and creative nonfiction. And we offer workshops with our authors and other artists.

Every writer and every publisher has a slant. Ours tilts toward the richness of the high desert, where all are welcome who manage to find their way.

We are proudly centered somewhere near Abiquiu, New Mexico. Visit us at casaurracaltd.com for exquisite and limited editions of our books, and for workshop registration.

CPSIA information can be obtained
at www.ICGtesting.com
Printed in the USA
FSHW011253291021
85764FS